DARK SIDE OF THE BEAN

SHOWCASE
Roli Books

SHOWCASE
A Roli Books imprint for titles sponsored by individuals or organizations.

Published in India by Roli Books
M-75, Greater Kailash II Market
New Delhi-110 048, India
Phone: ++91-11-4068 2000
Email: info@rolibooks.com
Website: www.rolibooks.com

ISBN: 978-81-942068-0-4

Design: Maanasa Ganesh
Project management: Elizabeth Verghese

Printed and bound at
EIH Press, Manesar

DARK SIDE OF THE BEAN

150 Sweet Temptations

KUMUD DWIVEDI

ACKNOWLEDGEMENTS

But for the countless people who helped along the way, encouraged me to experiment and walk the road less travelled, this book would have remained a distant dream. It would be impossible for me to list all the names but do please consider this a personal note of thanks.

I fall short of words to express my gratitude to my parents … I miss you both dearly as I put together the finishing touches to a dream I shared with you decades ago.

To my sister, Payal, and my brother, Pasha… thanks for putting up with endless tasting sessions and always appreciating my efforts.

To my aunt Toshi… but for your first lessons of encouragement, I wonder if I would have reached anywhere.

My dear friends Lovely, Vanduta, Seema, Priya, Fabia and Christin … your constructive feedback always encouraged me to do better.

Alfons and Christoph Wachter… agreeing to let me intern with you in Austria and introducing me to the commercial aspects of baking and pastry making was a key milestone of my journey.

To the chefs across the world with whom I trained or collaborated, thank you for being my torchbearers.

A special thanks to Mr. Radhakrishnan Nair for teaching me the finer intricacies of Food Photography.

And most of all, thanks to Nishant, my son, and Praveen, my husband … you have been my pillars of unconditional support on this journey, keeping up with the highs and lows, the good and bad. Without you both, my life would be incomplete.

Finally, a thank you to Maanasa and Liz for helping me put together my debut cookbook. Hope to work with you on few more!

Bangalore – 2020

FOR MY SON, NISHANT

'Love is the bridge between you and everything'
Rumi

KUMUD DWIVEDI

My journey from a somewhat sane person to a dessert-obsessed insomniac began in my childhood and continues to this day. For me, baking is magical. Desserts are homage to the perfect combination of science and creativity.

Born to a Punjabi family in India, food was the centre of our lives and dessert a necessary part of finishing a meal. As a young girl, I have distinct memories of happily helping my mother in her culinary chores but I knew that there was more to discover. I spent my pocket money buying endless second-hand international food magazines sold on the streets of Delhi. Baking, especially western desserts, was a very rare art those years. I pored over the magazines and whatever I prepared was greatly appreciated by family and friends, though I distinctly remember times when some of the ingredients were not available and the desserts were inedible!

Thinking that my obsession with baking was a passing fancy, I was advised to pick a more mainstream career. I lasted in the corporate world for just about a decade and during a sabbatical, when my son was born, I decided to say goodbye to corporate life and follow my dream.

I set up a small exclusive patisserie in the city of Kolkata, which is already famed for its local Bengali sweet delicacies, but it seemed to click. When we moved to Bangalore, I dived into studying; over the years, I completed the Chocolate and Patisserie courses at Ecole Nationale Supérieure de la Pâtisserie in France, the ZDS in Germany and trained at the Christophe Morel Academy in Canada. I was fortunate to intern with Alfons Wachter, a third-generation baker in Zams, near Innsbruck, Austria; meet and collaborate over periods of time with senior bakers in Spain and the Netherlands; work with amazingly talented chefs in America, Europe, Canada, Thailand, UAE and, of course, India.

This book is a collage of happy memories and a tribute to all the people I have worked with or learnt from, and the countless desserts I have eaten, offered and relished over the years.

I hope you enjoy the journey as much as I've done. This is only the start!

Kumud Dwivedi

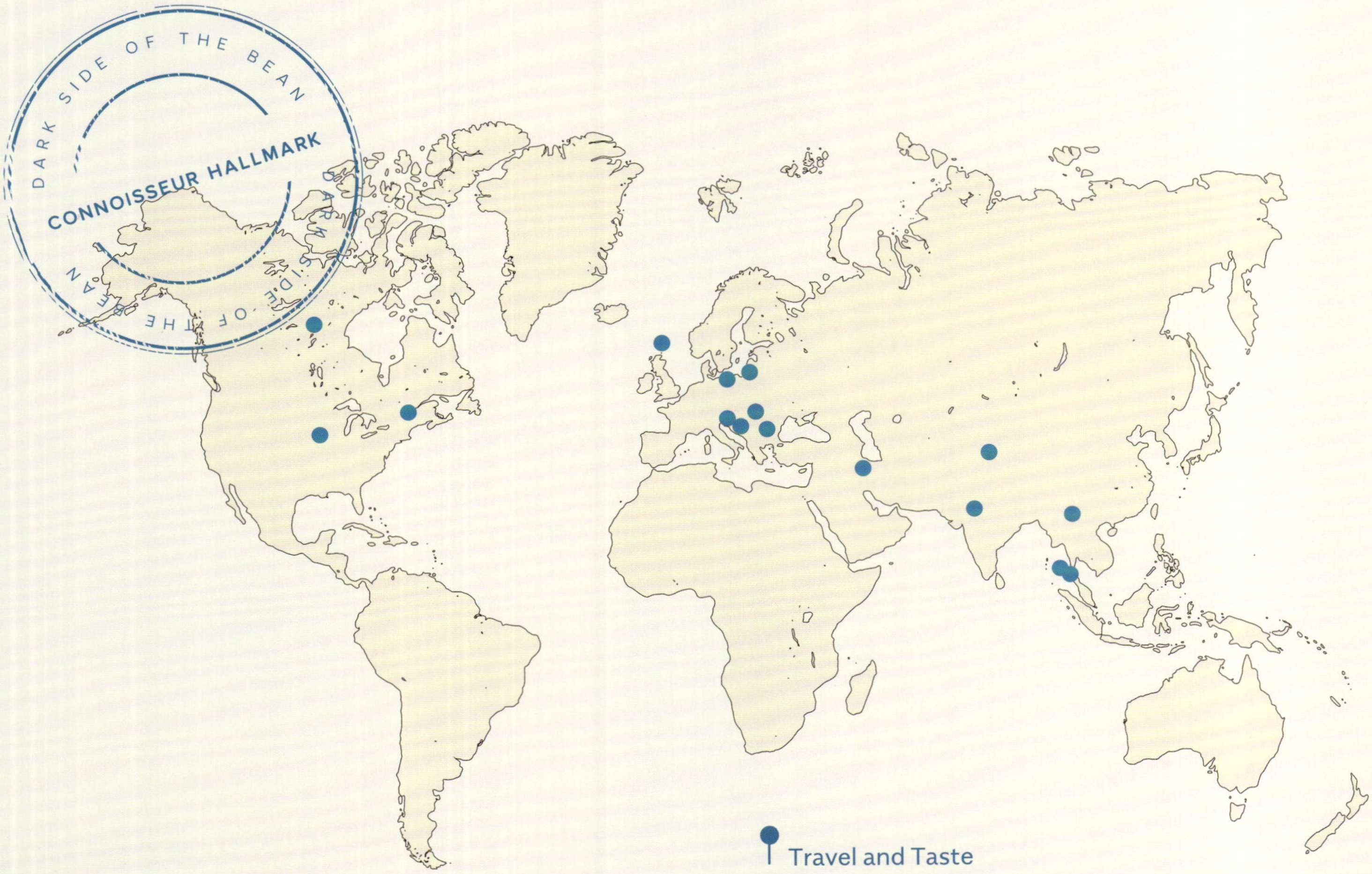

Travel and Taste

Austria, Belgium, Canada, France, Germany, Greece, Italy, Malaysia, Mauritius, Nepal, Netherlands, Portugal, Singapore, Slovenia, Spain, Sri Lanka, Switzerland, Thailand, UAE, UK, USA.

In keeping with Kumud's penchant for food and travel, a stamp seemed like the perfect icon for her debut gourmet dessert book. After all, stamps or hallmarks often denote quality, and like her recipes, a stamp could impress the taste buds; imprint a sensation in one's memory and most of all it could celebrates the chef's wanderlust along with her collecting and innovating a variety of delectable treats.

After years of training, testing and refining her craft, Kumud has put together an eclectic mix of tried and tested recipes, creating extraordinary sensations by combining the sweet with a hint of spice. A stamp of her uniqueness!

While this book may contain a few recipes not necessarily for the novice, it certainly should not stop anyone from starting on their baking adventure. Enjoy!

Anytime Is Cookie Time!

ROUGH AND TUMBLE COOKIES

Yield – 8/10 cookies

All-purpose flour – 100 gms
Rice flour – 45 gms
Baking powder – ¼ tsp
Salt – ⅛ teaspoon
Unsalted butter, soft – 180 gms
Brown sugar – 125 gms
Vanilla extract – 5 gms
Rolled oats – 120 gms
Coarse brown sugar, for sprinkling – 50 gm

Sift the all-purpose flour, rice flour, baking powder and salt and keep aside.

Beat the butter in a bowl of a stand mixer on low speed for three minutes. Add the brown sugar and beat on moderately low speed for one minute. Blend in the vanilla extract. Blend in the rolled oats and the sifted flour mix on low speed.

Pour the dough into a 26 cm tart pan and lightly press in an even layer without compressing it too much. Sprinkle the coarse sugar evenly over the top.

Bake the shortbread at 180°C in a preheated oven for 30 minutes, or until set and evenly medium golden on top. Cool the shortbread in the pan for 10 minutes then remove from tin & cool completely. Cut into approximately 8-10 wedges. Store in an airtight container.

BLACK AND WHITE COOKIES

Yield – 20 cookies

Cookies
Cocoa nibs – 45 gms
Unsalted butter – 180 gms
Baking soda – 1 tsp
Fleur de sel – ¼ tsp
Brown sugar – 125 gms
Caster sugar – 125 gms
Cocoa powder – 55 gms
Dark chocolate, 60-70%, melted – 180 gms
Pure vanilla extract – 15 ml
All-purpose flour – 235 gms

Filling
Caster sugar – 400 gms
Water – 125 ml
Fresh lemon juice – ½ tsp
Liquid glucose – 15 gms
Fleur de sel – a pinch
Seeds of 1 Vanilla bean

Cookies: Grind the cocoa nibs to a coarse consistency. In the bowl of a stand mixer, cream the butter, baking soda, salt and cocoa nibs on low speed for 2-3 minutes, until softened. Add the sugars and cocoa powder. Mix until the mixture is light and fluffy. Add the melted chocolate and vanilla extract, and mix for another minute. Fold the flour and mix on low speed, just to combine all the ingredients.

Divide the dough in equal halves. Place one half of the dough between two sheets of parchment paper and roll out to a 2 mm thickness. To remove the top parchment paper off the dough, transfer to a baking sheet and chill for five minutes. Roll out the other half of the dough in the same manner and chill.

Remove the top pieces of the parchment paper. Using a two inch round, fluted cookie cutter, cut out the circles. Place them half inch apart on parchment-lined baking sheets. Gather the remaining dough, roll this out again, and cut out the circles in the same manner. Using a decorative cookie stamp, create a pattern on each cookie.

Bake the cookies at 150°C in a preheated oven for about 25-30 minutes. Leave to cool.

Filling: In a heavy-duty saucepan, boil sugar, water, lemon juice, glucose, and salt. Cook the syrup until it reaches the soft-ball stage to 116°C.

Cool the syrup in the bowl of stand mixer with paddle attachment to 60°C. Beat on medium speed for 3-5 minutes, until it becomes white. Keep in a warm place.

Assembly: Flip half of the cookies over, so the patterned side is face down. Place the filling in a plastic pastry bag with a plain tip. Pipe a circle of filling around the perimeter of the flipped over cookie, about 5 mm away from the edge. Place the non-filled cookie over the filled one, creating a sandwich. Store in an airtight container.

APRICOT PISTA BUTTONS

Yield – 30 cookies

Pistachio cookies
All-purpose flour – 140 gms
Pistachios, shelled – 25 gms
Caster sugar – 75 gms
Fleur de sel – a pinch
Unsalted Butter, chilled – 125 gms
Egg – 1
Almond extract – ⅛ tsp
Zest of one lemon

Filling
Unsalted butter – 50 gms
White chocolate – 60 gms
Pistachios, finely slivered – 60 gms
Dried apricots, finely chopped – 4

Pistachio cookies: Blend the flour, pistachios, sugar, and salt in a food processor. Add the butter in pieces then process with on/off bursts until the mixture has the consistency of cornmeal. Whisk the egg, extract and zest in a small bowl. With the motor running pour the egg mixture down the feed tube and process just until ingredients are mixed to form a ball.

Shape the dough with the palms of the hand, level-measuring teaspoon at a time, into balls and set 1.5 cm apart on the baking sheet. Gently make an indentation in the centre of each ball, pressing down firmly without breaking through the dough.

Bake at 175°C in a preheated oven for 12 minutes or just until the cookies turn pale golden. Transfer to a wire rack to cool.

Filling: In a small saucepan, melt the butter and white chocolate, stirring just until chocolate is almost completely liquid. Place ¼ teaspoon white chocolate butter mix into each of the cookie indentations. Sprinkle the slivered pistachios and apricots over chocolate. Allow 30 minutes to set.

Store in an airtight metal container.

HAZELNUT PEBBLES

Yield – 24 cookies

Icing sugar – 75 gms
Unsalted butter, soft – 150 gms
Seeds of 1 Vanilla bean
Grated zest of 1 orange
Eggs – 2
All-purpose flour – 200 gms
Hazelnuts, ground – 50 gms
Cocoa powder – 15 gms
Dark chocolate 60-70%, tempered – 250 gms
Cocoa nibs, to sprinkle – 50 gms
Hazelnuts, toasted and chopped, to sprinkle – 50 gms

Put the sugar and butter in the bowl of a stand mixer with paddle attachment and beat until pale and fluffy. Add the orange zest and vanilla seeds and beat in. Gradually beat in the eggs until well incorporated. Gently fold in the flour, ground hazelnuts and cocoa powder with a large spatula. Bring the dough together into a ball using hands. Wrap in cling film and refrigerate for about one hour.

Take the dough out of the refrigerator and put on a lightly floured surface. Using a rolling pin, spread out until about 5 mm thick. Stamp out rounds with the 4 cm round cookie cutter and arrange on a parchment lined baking sheet.

Bake at 170°C a preheated oven for ten minutes. Remove the sablés from the oven and let it cool completely on the baking sheet.

Dip half of each sable in the tempered chocolate and sprinkle chopped hazelnuts and cocoa nibs over the top. Allow to set before serving.

PEANUT STAMP COOKIES

Yield – 20 cookies

Unsalted butter, soft – 120 gms
Peanut butter – 120 gms
Caster sugar – 50 gms
Honey – 3 tbsp
Fleur de sel – ¼ tsp
Baking soda – ½ tsp
Vanilla extract – 1 tsp
All-purpose flour – 175 gms
Oat flour – 100 gms

The beauty of these cookies lies in finding old molds to stamp patterns.

Beat together everything except the flours until well combined. Gently stir in the flours until just incorporated. If the dough is dry and crumbly, stir in about one tablespoon (or less) of water to bring it together. Divide the dough in half, shape each half into a disc, and cover with cling film. Refrigerate for at least one hour.

Working with one disc at a time, place the dough on a lightly floured surface and roll 3-4 mm thick. Dip the cookie stamps into flour, then press into the dough. Using a 7.5 cm fluted round cutter, cut out stamped cookies and transfer them to the parchment-lined trays. Bake the cookies at 180°C in a preheated oven for 8 to 10 minutes, until lightly golden. Repeat with the remaining dough.

Remove the cookies from the oven and let them cool completely.

ANZAC HONEY COOKIES

Yield – 24 cookies

Unsalted butter – 125 gms
Honey – 20 gms
Water – 40 ml
Rolled oats – 100 gms
Caster sugar – 215 gms
All-purpose flour – 150 gms
Coconut, dried, shredded – 70 gms
Baking soda – 1½ tsp

Place butter, honey and water in a small saucepan over medium heat until the butter has melted. Stir to combine, then set aside until the mixture has cooled. Place the remaining ingredients in a large bowl and blend well with a whisk. Pour in the melted butter mixtuare and stir until all the ingredients are evenly combined but not over-mixed.

Roll dessertspoons of the mixture into balls the size of a walnut. Place the balls on the baking trays, allowing plenty of room for spreading, and bake at 160°C in a preheated oven for 10-15 minutes or until the biscuits are lightly golden.

Allow the biscuits to cool on the trays for five minutes, then transfer to wire racks to cool completely. The biscuits become crisp on cooling.

LEBANESE TREATS

Yield – 20 cookies

Ghee (Indian clarified butter) – 100 gms
Icing sugar – 35 gms
All-purpose flour – 185 gms
Salt – ½ tsp
Orange blossom water – 4 tsp
Rose water – 3 tsp
Unsalted pistachios, for topping

This recipe is a version of the Lebanese shortbread, commonly known as Ghraybeh, pronounced ghri (like high)-bee.

Keep the ghee in refrigerator till it sets.

Sift the flour and salt and keep aside. In a stand mixer fitted with the paddle attachment, cream together the ghee and icing sugar for five minutes, until fluffy, creamy, and pale. Fold in the flour, salt, orange blossom and rose water and mix for a good 3 to 4 minutes, until a uniform, smooth dough forms. Wrap the dough in plastic wrap and chill for one hour.

Pinch a piece of dough, weighing about 15 gms, and roll it into a ball between the palms. Flatten it slightly and place on a baking sheet lined with the parchment paper. Repeat with the rest of the dough, arranging the cookies on lined sheets and spacing them well apart. Press one pistachio into the centre of each cookie.

Bake at 180°C in a preheated oven for 15 minutes, making sure the cookies don't take on any color but nevertheless cook through. Remove from the oven when done and leave to cool down completely.

ALMOND AMORE

Yield – 24 cookies

All-purpose flour – 140 gms
Almond flour – 40 gms
Baking powder – ⅛ tsp
Fleur de sel – a pinch
Unsalted butter, soft – 125 gms
Caster sugar – 100 gms
Large egg, separated – 1
Grated zest of ½ lemon
Vanilla extract – ½ tsp
Almonds, sliced, blanched – 100 gms

Mix flour, almond flour, baking powder, and salt and set aside. Using a stand mixer fitted with the paddle attachment beat together the butter and sugar on medium speed until light and fluffy, about 2 minutes. Beat in the egg yolk, followed by the lemon zest and vanilla extract. Beat in the flour mix on low speed to make a stiff dough. Remove the dough from the bowl, flatten it into a disc, wrap it in plastic, and chill until it is firm enough to roll; about one hour.

Place the almonds in a shallow bowl. In another shallow bowl, lightly beat the egg white with a fork until frothy.

Divide the dough into three equal pieces. Roll each piece of dough into a narrow log 8 mm in diameter. Cut the log into cylinders about 4 cm long. Roll each cylinder in the beaten egg white, then in the sliced almonds to coat it completely. Place the cookies on the parchment lined baking trays, spacing them evenly.

Bake the cookies at 160°C in a preheated oven until they are firm and the almonds are lightly golden brown; about 14 to 16 minutes. Allow the cookies to cool on the sheets for 1 or 2 minutes, and then use a spatula to remove them gently to a wire rack to cool completely. If desired, dust with icing sugar.

CHOCO CHUNK COOKIES

Yield – 18 cookies

All-purpose flour – 100 gms
Baking soda – 2.5 gms
Fleur de sel – ¼ tsp
Dark chocolate, 60-70%, roughly chopped – 175 gms
Seeds of ½ Vanilla bean
Unsalted butter, soft – 70 gms
Caster sugar – 60 gms
Brown sugar – 60 gms
Eggs – 1
Maldon sea salt – 5 gms

Sift the flour with baking soda and salt and keep aside. In a stand mixer fitted with the paddle attachment, at high speed, combine the butter, the vanilla seeds, and both sugars; beat until fully mixed and the color pales to a lighter shade. As soon as the color changes, lower the speed of the mixer and add the egg beat until fully incorporated. Add the sifted flour and mix until just incorporated. Add chopped chocolate (reserving a few for topping) and mix till combined.

Scoop 5 cm balls of the dough onto the parchment lined baking sheet, spacing them well apart. Sprinkle each cookie with a few flakes of sea salt and place a few pieces of chocolate on top of each ball. Bake at 180°C in a preheated oven for ten minutes till the centre is gooey and the edges are crispy. Slam the baking sheet against the counter immediately on taking out from oven to remove any air bubbles. Use a metal spatula to set the warm cookies on a cooling rack, and let cool for 5 to 10 minutes.

HAZELNUT COFFEE BISCUITS

Yield – 50 cookies

Biscuits
Unsalted butter – 125 gms
Caster sugar – 125 gms
Zest of 1 lemon
Egg yolk – 1
Lemon juice – 1 tsp
Hazelnut powder – 125 gms
All-purpose flour – 155 gms

Icing
Icing sugar, sifted – 125 gms
Unsalted butter, melted – 30 gms
Lemon juice – 3-4 tsp

Coffee cream
Caster sugar – 125 gms
Water – 60 ml
Instant coffee powder – 1 tbsp
Unsalted butter, soft – 80 gms

Biscuits: Beat the butter and sugar in a mixing bowl until light and creamy. Add the zest, egg yolk, juice and hazelnut powder. Beat until well combined. Fold in the sifted flour. Shape the dough into a smooth ball and cover in plastic wrap. Refrigerate for 20 minutes.

Divide the dough in half. Roll one portion between two sheets of baking paper until ¼ inch thick. Using an oval fluted cutter cut out the shapes and place on parchment lined baking trays. Repeat the above process with remaining dough. Bake for ten minutes at 170°C in a preheated oven until the biscuits are golden. Remove from oven and transfer to wire racks to cool.

Icing: Combine icing sugar and butter in a mixing bowl. Add enough lemon juice to form a smooth mixture. Place into a piping paper bag. Snip off the tip. Pipe the icing onto each biscuit.

Coffee cream: Combine the sugar, water and coffee in a pan. Stir over low heat without boiling, until the sugar dissolves. Bring to the boil; reduce heat and simmer uncovered for 4-5 minutes without stirring. Beat butter in a mixing bowl until light and creamy. Pour cooled syrup in a thin stream beating constantly until thick and glossy. Place in piping bag with star tip and pip small rosettes on top of the iced biscuits.

MOLASSES COOKIES

Yield – 36 cookies

Unsalted butter – 225 gms
All-purpose flour – 275 gms
Baking soda – 10 gms
Fleur de sel – ¼ tsp
Cinnamon powder – 1 tsp
Clove powder – ½ tsp
Ginger powder – ½ tsp
Caster sugar – 170 gms
Unsulphured molasses – 80 gms
Egg – 1
Caster sugar – 60 gms (for rolling the dough balls)

Unlike refined sugar, which has zero nutritional value, blackstrap molasses contains some vitamins and minerals.

In a medium heavy saucepan over very low heat, melt the butter. Increase the heat to low and cook, uncovered, watching carefully to prevent burning. Remove any foam on the surface to check the progress. As soon as the milk solids become a deep brown, immediately pour through the strainer into the measure, reserving the browned solids.

Measure 145 gms of the butter and add the browned solids to it. Let it cool to 27°C. Sift the flour, baking soda, salt, cinnamon, cloves, and ginger powder and set aside. In the bowl of a stand mixer fitted with paddle attachment, mix the clarified butter, sugar, molasses, and egg on low speed for one minute. Add the flour mixture. Keep the speed to low and beat for 30 seconds. Make a round ball of the dough and wrap in cling film. Refrigerate for one hour, or until firm enough to handle.

Scoop out a heaping tablespoon of dough. Make a ball and roll it around in the sugar to coat it well. Set the dough balls on parchment-lined trays, each a minimum 5 cm inches apart from the next. Bake 170°C in preheated oven for about ten minutes till they are flat and slightly under baked. Cool the cookies on the tray and after five minutes transfer them to a wire rack. These will crisp up after cooling.

NUTELLA SKILLET COOKIES

Yield – 4 cookies

Cookies
All-purpose flour – 100 gms
Baking powder – ¾ tsp
Salt – ¼ tsp
Rolled oats – 40 gms
Unsalted butter, soft – 125 gms
Light brown sugar – 150 gms
Egg – 1
Vanilla extract – 1 tsp
Chocolate-hazelnut spread, such as Nutella – 150 gms

Topping
Dark chocolate chunks – 60 gms
Rolled oats – 20 gms
Fleur de sel – ¼ tsp

Old English toffee ice cream
Caster sugar – 185 gms
Egg yolks – 5
Cream 35% (A) – 250 gms
Cream 35% (B) – 430 gms
Vanilla extract – 1 tsp

Cookies: Grease 4 mini skillets of 12 cm diameter. Whisk together flour, baking powder, and salt. Stir in oats. Set aside. Beat the butter and brown sugar until light and fluffy. Add the egg and vanilla, and mix well. Reduce mixer speed to low. Gradually, add flour mixture, mixing until just combined. Set aside about ½ cup of dough. Divide remaining dough among the prepared skillets, spreading evenly and firmly in the bottom of each skillet. Top each with about two tablespoons of chocolate-hazelnut spread, and smear evenly.

Drop the ½ cup of dough by teaspoonful over the chocolate-hazelnut spread. Sprinkle with chocolate chunks and oats. Sprinkle a pinch of salt on each cookie. Place the skillets on a baking sheet. Bake cookies at 160°C in a preheated oven, for 35 to 40 minutes or until the cookies are golden brown. Cool for about ten minutes before topping with ice cream.

Old English toffee ice cream: In a small saucepan, cook 100 gms sugar over low heat until a dark golden brown. Pour cream (A) into sugar. Stir to prevent boiling over. When cream is piping hot and caramel has completely melted, pour over the three whisked egg yolks. Beat well; then cool. Churn in ice cream machine. Freeze.

In a heatproof bowl, whisk 85 gms sugar and remaining two egg yolks until thick and smooth. In a small saucepan, scald cream (B). Add vanilla; pour over eggs. Place the bowl over a pan of simmering water. Stir slowly and continually until custard coats back of spoon. Cool. Churn in ice cream machine. Stir frozen ice creams together to get marble effect.

for tea

CURRANT & HAZELNUT BISCUITS

Yield – 20 cookies

All-purpose flour – 175 gms
Brown sugar – 40 gms
Fleur de sel – ½ tsp
Baking powder – 1 tsp
Rolled oats – 25 gms
Unsalted butter – 75 gms
Milk – 60 ml
Dried currants – 40 gms
Roasted hazelnuts, roughly chopped – 40 gms
Fleur de sel, to sprinkle

This process of making a log of the dough and then slicing allows all add-ons to be visible once the cookie is baked.

Place the flour, sugar, salt, baking powder and oats in a mixer with a paddle attachment. Add the diced butter and beat at slow speed until you have a rough breadcrumb consistency. Use just enough of the milk to form a dough and then mix in the dried fruits and nuts.

Roll into logs about 20 cm long. Wrap each in cling film and then place in the fridge to set for at least an hour.

Take the dough logs out of the fridge, remove cling film and slice them into thin discs (about 1 cm). Lay them flat on the parchment lined baking trays, allowing 2 cm between each and sprinkle with the salt.

Bake at 170°C in a preheated oven, for 15 minutes, until the biscuits are golden. Cool on a rack, and then store in an airtight container.

SWEDISH MAFIA COOKIES

Yield – 20 cookies

Cookies
Unsalted butter, soft – 80 gms
Caster sugar – 135 gms
Egg – 1
Vanilla extract – 1 tsp
All-purpose flour – 175 gms
Baking powder – 1 tsp
Cinnamon powder – 1 tsp

Topping
Walnuts chopped – 50 gms
Cinnamon powder – 2 tbsp
Caster sugar – 30 gms

For a change, the spice-nut combination for the topping can be played with.

Cookies: In a large bowl, cream butter and sugar. Beat in the egg and vanilla until light. Sift flour with baking powder and cinnamon. Add to the creamed mixture, blending well. Chill dough for 30 minutes. Remove dough from fridge and shape into balls the size of walnuts. Roll each ball in the walnut-cinnamon topping. Place on baking sheets lined with parchment about 6 cm apart. Bake cookies at 130°C in a preheated oven for 10 to 12 minutes until golden.

Topping: Mix the walnuts, cinnamon, and sugar in a small bowl and keep ready to cover the cookies before baking.

CHOCOLATE MUD FLAPS

Yield – 12 cookies

Sable
Egg yolks – 3
Caster sugar – 100 gms
Unsalted butter – 125 gms
Seeds of 1 Vanilla bean
Fleur de sel – a pinch
All-purpose flour – 250 gms
Baking powder – 2 tsp

Praline
Hazelnuts – 150 gms
Caster sugar – 150 gms
Hazelnut oil – 1 tsp

Finishing
Hazelnuts, roasted, chopped – 30 gms
Dark chocolate, tempered

Sable: Mix flour, salt and baking powder in a food processor. Add the butter and mix.

Whisk egg yolks, sugar and vanilla. Add to above and make a ball of the dough. Cover with cling film and leave to rest for 30 minutes in refrigerator. Roll to 8 mm thickness and cut 6 cm rounds and arrange on a baking sheet. Again leave to rest for one hour in the fridge. Remove from refrigerator and bake at 170°C in a preheated oven for 12-15 minutes.

Praline: Spread the nuts out on a baking tray lined with parchment and roast at 190°C in a preheated oven for 8-10 minutes until lightly golden. Transfer roasted nuts to a heavy-based saucepan. Cook over a medium heat while gradually adding the sugar and stirring continuously. Continue to cook and stir until the sugar turns an amber caramel, about 15-18 minutes. Pour the caramelised nuts onto a baking tray lined with a silicone mat and leave to cool. When the nuts have cooled, break up the praline and transfer it to a heavy-duty blender. Add the hazelnut oil. Blitz until you have a smooth paste.

Spread some praline paste on top of the cookies. Sprinkle with chopped hazelnuts on top. Let it set in fridge. Enrobe with tempered dark chocolate.

TOASTED SNOW COOKIES

Yield – 30 cookies

Coconut spritz dough
Coconut, dried,
shredded – 40 gms
All-purpose flour – 160 gms
Fleur de sel – ½ tsp
Unsalted butter, soft – 120 gms
Icing sugar – 60 gms
Coconut cream – 60 gms
Vanilla extract – 1 tsp

Dipping
Dark chocolate 60-70%, melted,
for dipping
Coconut, dried, shredded
to sprinkle

Coconut spritz dough Roast coconut on a baking sheet at 180°C, in a preheated oven, for about 5 minutes and then cool. Mix the flour and shredded coconut and keep aside. In the bowl of a stand mixer fitted with the paddle attachment, mix the butter and sugar and beat for 3-4 minutes until the butter mixture is aerated. On medium speed, add coconut cream and vanilla and continue to mix for another 20 to 30 seconds to make the dough nearly homogeneous. With the mixer on low speed, gradually add coconut-flour mixture. Mix until the dough just comes together. Do not over mix. If the dough seems too thick to pipe, mix in a little coconut cream.

Fill the pastry bag with a large star tip. Pipe 8 cm-long sticks onto the parchment lined pans, allowing 5 cm of space between each cookie. Chill for 15 to 20 minutes. Then bake the cookies at 180°C for about 10-15 minutes, in a preheated oven, until the cookies brown around the edges and hold their shape when touched. Let the cookies cool completely in the pan.

Dipping: Dip the ends of the cookies into the melted chocolate, shake off any excess, and place on parchment-lined pan. Sprinkle shredded coconut over the melted chocolate. Store in an airtight container.

ORANGE WAFERS

Yield – 30 cookies

Unsalted butter – 500 gms
Rye flakes – 125 gms
Caster sugar – 250 gms
Eggs – 2
All-purpose flour – 2 tsp
Baking powder – 2 tsp
Orange zest – 2 tsp
Fleur de sel – a pinch

The wafers are ideal when thin and translucent.

Melt the butter and mix it with the rye flakes in a bowl. Stir in the sugar and eggs. In another bowl, mix the flour, baking powder, orange zest and salt. Stir this into the rye mixture. Use two teaspoons to drop small mounds of the mixture on to a baking tray lined with baking parchment, spacing them out well. Bake at 180°C in a preheated oven for about ten minutes, then leave to cool. After cooling use a palette knife to transfer them to a wire rack. Store in an airtight container.

CHOCOMEL COOKIES

Yield – 30 cookies

Caramel
Cream, 35% – 120 gms
Unsalted butter – 45 gms
Seeds of ½ Vanilla bean
Liquid Glucose – 30 gms
Caster sugar – 200 gms

Ganache
Caster sugar – 30 gms
Liquid glucose – 30 gms
Water – 60 ml
Cocoa powder – 40 gms
Instant coffee – 1 tsp
Dark chocolate, 60-70% – 120 gms
Dark rum – 1 tbsp

Cookies
Unsalted butter – 250 gms
Fleur De sel – ½ tsp
Caster sugar – 100 gms
Brown sugar – 70 gms
Cocoa powder – 50 gms
Corn flour – 30 gms
Egg yolks – 2
Vanilla extract – 1 tsp
All-purpose flour – 275 gms

Topping
Fleur de sel
Cocoa powder
Gold powder

Caramel: Heat cream, butter and vanilla seeds until the butter melts and keep aside. In a small heavy-duty saucepan, over medium heat, cook the glucose until its bubbly. Add a tablespoon or so of the sugar, stirring constantly. When the sugar has melted completely add the next tablespoon of sugar. Continue in this manner until all the sugar has been added. Cook for 3-4 more minutes, stirring and swirling the pan until the caramel is thick and has turned a light-golden brown.

Remove the caramel from the heat, and stir in the butter-and-cream mixture. Return the saucepan to medium heat, and cook the caramel for another 3-5 minutes, until it has turned a deep golden-brown colour. Transfer the caramel to a bowl and cool completely.

Ganache: Heat sugar, glucose, water, cocoa powder and coffee over medium heat. Bring the mixture to a boil for 1-2 minutes, stirring constantly to prevent it from burning at the bottom. Remove the pan from the heat, and whisk in the chocolate. Bring the mixture back to a boil, and reduce heat for a minute or so, whisking constantly, until the chocolate is completely melted. Remove the pan from the heat and stir in the rum. The mixture should be shiny and smooth. Transfer it to a bowl and cool at room temperature.

Cookies: In the bowl of a stand mixture fitted with the paddle attachment, cream the butter and salt on low speed for 2-3 minutes, until softened. Add the sugars, and mix on medium speed until the mixture is light and fluffy. Mix cocoa powder and cornstarch on low, and beat for a minute to incorporate. Add egg yolks and vanilla and beat on low speed. Add flour and mix. Divide the dough in half and flatten into two discs. Chill it for about 15 minutes, until firm.

Remove one half of the dough from the refrigerator. On a lightly floured surface, roll the dough out to 3 mm thickness. Cut circles of 5 cm diameters. Place them 10 cm apart on a parchment-lined baking sheet. Use this set as the bottom half of the sandwich. Remove the second half of the dough from the refrigerator. Roll it out, cut out the cookies, and place them on a baking sheet in the same manner as before. Now using a 2 cm round cookie cutter, cut out the centres of this layer of cookies. Chill both the top and bottom layer cookies for 10 minutes.

Bake at 170°C in a preheated oven for about 15 minutes. Allow cookies to cool completely. Flip one layer of the cookies over using a piping bag fitted with a plain tip, pipe a ring of the caramel 5 mm from the edge, leaving the circular centre for the ganache. Fill the centres of the cookies with the ganache.

Sift a fine layer of cocoa powder over the cookie tops. Centre the tops over the bottom layer of cookies, cocoa-powder side facing up. Sprinkle the ganache in the centre with a few grains of fleur de sel and decorate with some gold powder.

CHOCOMEL COOKIES

ALMOND CIGARS

Yield – 36 cookies

Egg whites – 3
Caster sugar – 100 gms
All-purpose flour – 45 gms
Unsalted butter, melted – 75 gms
Vanilla extract – 1 tsp
Sliced almonds – 50 gms

Grease Teflon-coated baking sheets with a thin layer of butter. In a large mixing bowl, whisk the whites with the sugar just until foamy. Whisk in the flour, and then the butter and vanilla until well blended. Drop teaspoonfuls of batter quite apart on a baking sheet. Tap the baking sheet on the work surface to spread the batter slightly. Sprinkle a few sliced almonds on each disk.

Bake, one sheet at a time, for eight minutes or just until the edges are golden with ivory-colored centres. Place baking sheet on a wire rack to cool for only 15 seconds. With a metal spatula, lift the cookies one at a time, and lay over a rolling pin to curve each cookie while it is still warm and pliable. The cookies will become crisp as they cool. Stack in an airtight metal container and store at room temperature.

EMOJI COOKIES

Yield – 20 cookies

Graham crackers
Unsalted butter, soft – 250 gms
Coconut sugar – 165 gms
Honey – 1 tsp
Vanilla extract – 1 tsp
All-purpose flour – 210 gms
Whole wheat flour – 125 gms
Wheat bran – 30 gms
Baking powder – 1 tsp
Salt – ¼ tsp
Ground cinnamon – 1 tsp

Ganache
Dark chocolate 60-70% – 150 gms
Cream 35% – 60 gms
Sugar – 15 gms
Fleur de sel – a pinch
Peanut butter – 125 gms

Graham crackers: Mix butter, coconut sugar, honey and vanilla in the bowl of a stand mixer with the paddle attachment for two minutes at high speed.

In a separate bowl, sift all the dry ingredients and add to the above mixture. Mix briefly to obtain a homogeneous paste. Put the dough between two sheets of parchment paper and using a rolling pin, roll the dough to approximately 3 mm thick. Keep in the fridge for two hours.

Cut into shapes. Make cut outs in half of the cookies (as indicated in image). Bake at 180°C in a preheated oven for about 10 minutes.

Ganache: Boil cream, sugar and salt. Pour over chocolate and peanut butter. Start blending from the centre with hand blender to get a smooth and shiny ganache. Put in a piping bag and pipe with a plain tip on the bottom of the plain cookies. Cover with cutout cookies.

PINK PEPPERCORN SHORTBREAD

Yield – 12 cookies

Unsalted butter, cold – 140 gms
Caster sugar – 125 gms
Fleur de sel – a pinch
Egg yolks, hard boiled – 2
Seeds of 1 Vanilla bean
All-purpose flour – 185 gms
Egg – 1

For garnishing
Pink peppercorns – 20 gms
Coarse sea salt

Put the butter, sugar and salt in the bowl of stand mixer with the paddle attachment and beat on medium-low speed until a sugary paste forms with no visible lumps of butter. Press the egg-yolks through a fine mesh strainer into a bowl. Add the yolks and vanilla seeds to the butter and mix until well incorporated. Turn the mixer to low and gradually add the flour. Mix until just incorporated. Use a rolling pin to roll the dough 2 cm thick between two sheets of parchment. Transfer the dough to a sheet pan and freeze until firm, at least one hour. Remove the dough from the freezer and let stand for 10 minutes. When partially thawed, roll the dough again between the parchment sheets until it is 1.5 cm thick.

Use either a 5 cm plain round cutter or a 5 cm square cutter to cut dough shapes and transfer them to the parchment lined baking trays, about 1 inch apart. Reroll the scraps and cut cookies until the dough is used up. Cover the pans and freeze for 30 minutes, until ready to bake. Remove the cookies from the freezer and brush them with the beaten egg. Sprinkle pink peppercorns over the top along with a few flakes of coarse salt. Bake cookies at 180°C in a preheated oven until the edges of the cookies are a light golden brown. Cool for ten minutes in the pan before transferring to a rack to cool completely. Store in an airtight container.

CHOCOLATE SMOOCHIES

Yield – 24 cookies

Cookies
Almond powder,
toasted – 50 gms
All-purpose flour – 200 gms
Cocoa powder – 40 gms
Baking powder – ¼ tsp
Fleur de sel – ½ tsp
Unsalted butter, soft – 250 gms
Icing sugar – 125 gms
Vanilla extract – 2 tsp
Dark rum – 1 tbsp

Ganache filling
Dark chocolate 60-70% –
240 gms
Unsalted butter,
soft – 15 gms
Cream 35% – 180 gms
Kahlua – 2 tsp
Granulated sugar, for rolling

Cookies: Sift together the flour, cocoa powder, baking powder, and salt and set aside.

Using a stand mixer fitted with the paddle attachment, beat together the butter and icing sugar on medium speed until creamy and light, about two minutes, then beat in the vanilla extract and rum, occasionally scraping down the sides of the bowl. On low speed, beat in the dry ingredients, followed by the almond powder. Remove the dough from the bowl, flatten into a disk, wrap it in cling film, and chill for about one hour.

Line two baking sheets with parchment paper. Divide the dough in 48 portions. Roll each portion into a ball and then roll in granulated sugar to coat them completely. Place the cookies on the prepared baking sheets, spaced a little apart.

Bake the cookies at 160°C in a preheated oven for 12 to 15 minutes until slight cracks appear on top. Allow the cookies to cool on the sheets for 1 to 2 minutes, and then use a spatula to remove them gently to a wire rack to cool completely.

Ganache filling: Place the chocolate and butter into a medium bowl. Heat the heavy cream in a saucepan until it comes to a boil and pour it over the chocolate and butter. Allow the mixture to sit undisturbed for two minutes, and then whisk until smooth and glossy. Whisk in the Kahlua. Allow the ganache to cool, whisking occasionally until it is firm enough to pipe.

Assembly: Pair up the cookies according to size. Take one cookie from each pair and using a pastry bag fitted with a star tip, pipe a small amount of ganache onto the flat side, then place the second cookie on the ganache to form a sandwich; the two rounded tops of the cookies should be facing outward. Allow the ganache to firm up at room temperature or in the refrigerator if necessary.

MELT IN THE MOUTH COOKIES

Yield – 12 cookies

Caramel chips
Cream, 35% – 50 gms
Fleur de sel – a pinch
Liquid glucose – 30 gms
Caster sugar – 60 gms
Unsalted butter – 15 gms

Cookies
Unsalted butter, soft – 100 gms
Brown sugar – 160 gms
Eggs – 2
All-purpose flour – 160 gms
Baking powder – ¼ tsp
Fleur de sel – a pinch
Pecans, roughly chopped – 100 gms
Caramel chips – 100 gms
(recipe on right)

Extra caramel chips can be stored for cake and ice cream topping.

Caramel chips: Heat cream and salt and keep aside. Make a caramel with sugar and glucose. Deglaze with warm cream and salt. Cook to 135°C and spread on silicone mat to cool. Break into small uneven pieces.

Cookies: Sift flour and baking powder and keep aside. Beat butter and sugar till well mixed. Add eggs and mix again. Fold in sifted flour and pecans. Make balls and put on silicone mat, keeping some distance from each other. Press lightly and sprinkle with caramel chips. Bake at 190°C in a preheated oven for 5-7 minutes. Leave on tray to cool completely.

VANILLA PALMIERS

Yield – 35/40 cookies

All-purpose flour – 200 gms
Fleur de sel – ¼ tsp
Unsalted butter, cold – 225 gms
Cream 35% – 75 gms
Caster sugar – 100 gms
Seeds of 1 Vanilla bean

Mix the sugar and vanilla seeds and keep aside. In the bowl of a stand mixer fitted with the paddle attachment, combine the flour and salt at low speed. Add the butter, one-third at a time, and mix for just a few seconds. The mixture will be very crumbly with large pieces of butter in it. While continuing to mix at low speed, add the cream and mix until the dough starts to come together. (Large pieces of butter should still be visible.)

Scrape the dough onto a lightly floured work surface. Roll the dough into an 20 x 40 cm rectangle, dusting the dough with flour as needed. Arrange the dough with a short side closest to you. Brush off any excess flour on the dough with a pastry brush. Fold the bottom third up over the centre, and then fold the top third over this, as if you were folding a letter. The dough now has three layers. Rotate the dough 90 degrees, so that the short sides are at the top and bottom. Roll the dough out again to an 20 x 40 cm rectangle. Fold it again to make three layers. The dough has now been "turned" twice. Wrap the dough in cling film and refrigerate for 30 minutes.

Remove the dough from the refrigerator and place it so that the short ends are on top and bottom. Roll and fold the dough as before to make two more turns. Wrap the dough in plastic wrap and chill for at least one hour before forming the cookies.

Cut the dough into two rectangles. Wrap one piece in a cling film and refrigerate while you roll the other piece. Sprinkle a work surface liberally with some vanilla sugar and roll out the dough to a 20 x 40 cm rectangle, sprinkling it with more of the sugar as you go along to prevent sticking. Using a chef's knife, cut off the ragged edges from the long sides of the dough rectangle. With one of the long sides facing you, fold the dough in half lengthwise then unfold it (this will give you a reference line for folding the dough). Fold the long side over the other, as if you were closing a book. Place the log of dough on a baking sheet, cover with plastic wrap, and refrigerate. Repeat process with the second piece of dough and refrigerate for one hour. (Set aside the remaining vanilla sugar, which you will use later.) Cut the rough end off one of the dough logs. Cut the log into 8 mm slices and dredge the slices lightly with more vanilla sugar on both sides. Arrange the cookies, flat side down, on the baking sheet, lined with parchment spacing them 5 cm apart.

Bake at 190°C, in a preheated oven, for 12 to 15 minutes, until the undersides of the cookies are golden brown and caramelised. The tops will still be light colored. Using a metal spatula, flip each cookie on to a cooling rack and cool completely. Store in an airtight container.

CRUNCHY MUNCHIES

Yield – 12 cookies

Rolled oats – 165 gms
All-purpose flour – 220 gms
Coconut, dried,
shredded – 100 gms
Brown sugar – 210 gms
Cranberries, dried – 50 gms
Unsalted butter – 185 gms
Black treacle – 60 gms
Baking soda – 1½ tsp

Put the oats, flour, coconut and 175 gms brown sugar in a bowl. In a small bowl, combine the cranberries with the 60 ml boiling water. Add the rest (35 gms) sugar and stir until it has dissolved. Put the butter and treacle in a saucepan over low heat, stirring until the butter has melted. Add the cranberry mixture and stir to combine. Now add the baking soda and 45 ml of boiling water and while it is still foaming, add to the oats mixture. Mix together with a large spoon.

Roll into 12 balls and place on baking tray. Use a metal spatula to press the dough down into very thin discs. Bake at 160°C, in a preheated oven for 15-20 minutes or until firm and golden.

Transfer to a wire rack to cool.

SMALL TREATS

Bite Off More Than You Can Chew!

VIKING CAKES

Yield – 24 treats

All-purpose flour – 130 gms
Cardamom seeds, powdered – 1 tsp
Baking powder – ¼ tsp
Unsalted butter, cold – 100 gms
Egg – 1
Lemon juice – 1 tsp
Water – ½ tbsp

Topping
Cold strong coffee to brush cookies
Granulated sugar
Almonds blanched, slivered

Traditionally called Jewish cookies, these are a Christmas staple in many Icelandic homes.

Mix the flour, cardamom, and baking powder in a food processor. Add butter and process until the mixture resembles coarse crumbs. Beat the egg with the lemon juice and two tablespoons water. Mix into the dry ingredients until dough starts to hold together, adding more water if necessary, one tablespoon at a time. Gather dough into a ball and chill for 30 minutes to one hour.

On a lightly floured board, roll dough out to about 3 mm thickness. Cut 5 cm rounds with a fluted cutter. Place on parchment lined baking sheets and brush with coffee; sprinkle with sugar and almonds. Bake at 180°C in a preheated oven for 10 to 12 minutes or until golden.

PLUM CELEBRATION

Yield – 12 treats

Plum and apple jam
Plum – 225 gms
Granny Smith apples – 225 gms
Water – 60 ml
Caster sugar – 225 gms
Cinnamon stick – 1
Seeds of 1 Vanilla bean

Vanilla cake
Unsalted butter, melted – 90 gms
Eggs – 2
Vanilla extract – ½ tsp
Fleur de sel – ¼ tsp
All-purpose flour – 200 gms
Sugar – 200 gms
Baking powder – 1 tsp
Milk – 125 ml

Plum jubilee buttercream
Water – 125 ml
Sugar – 225 gms
Liquid glucose – 20 gms
Cream of tartar – ¼ tsp
Egg yolks – 3
Xantana – ⅛ tsp
Unsalted butter, cubed – 340 gms
Syrup from plum and apple jam – 30 ml

Plum and apple jam: Remove the pits from the plums and coarsely chop. Peel, core and dice the apples. In a medium saucepan, cook plums, apples, water, cinnamon stick and vanilla seeds. Simmer for about 8 to 10 minutes till the fruit becomes soft. Stir in sugar and cook till thick and shiny. Remove cinnamon stick and leave to cool.

Vanilla cake: Line a 12 cupcake pan with paper liners. In a stand mixer with the paddle attachment, beat the eggs on medium-low speed for two minutes until light yellow and lightly foamy. Increase the mixer speed to medium-high. Pour the warm melted butter into the eggs slowly so that the mixture tempers and the eggs do not scramble. Once the butter is added, reduce the speed to medium-low.

With the mixer running, add the milk, vanilla, and salt. Mix for 1 minute until well combined. Stir together the flour, sugar, and baking powder and add to the batter. Mix on medium speed until just combined, 10 to 20 seconds.

Scoop the batter into the prepared baking cups, filling them two thirds of the way. Bake at 160°C in a preheated oven for 20 to 25 minutes. The cupcakes are done when the centres spring back when you touch them. Remove the cupcakes from the oven and allow to cool for five minutes, then place the cupcakes from the pan on to a baking sheet.

Plum jubilee buttercream: Heat water, sugar, glucose and cream of tartar in a heavy pan on a high heat. Bring to a boil and stir until the sugar is completely dissolved. Heat to 112°C . Put the yolks in a stand mixer with a whisk attachment and mix at high speed. Add Xantana when the syrup reaches 112°C; pour in a slow steady stream down the side of the bowl over the egg yolks. Whisk till cool. Now using a paddle attachment, add butter gradually on medium speed; once the butter is added increase the speed to medium-high for 20 seconds. Add the plum syrup and mix again. The mixture should be very fluffy.

Fill the buttercream in a pastry bag fitted with a star tip and pipe onto each vanilla cupcake. Top with some plum and apple jam.

COFFEE CHOCOLATE CAKES

Yield – 6 treats

Almond dacquoise
Egg whites – 8
Caster sugar – 85 gms
Almond powder – 200 gms
Icing sugar – 200 gms
Almonds, peeled, chopped & roasted – 40 gms

Coffee cream
Milk – 80 gms
Cream, 35% – 65 gms
Roasted coffee beans, crushed – 20 gms
Egg yolks – 3
Caster sugar – 45 gms
Gelatin powder – 4 gms
Cream, 35%, whipped – 165 gms

Chocolate mousse
Milk – 230 gms
Egg yolks – 3
Caster sugar – 130 gms
Dark chocolate, 60-70%, melted – 230 gms
Gelatin powder – 10 gms
Cream 35%, whipped – 500 gms

Milk chocolate glaze
Gelatin powder – 25 gms
Water – 125 gms
Caster sugar – 225 gms
Liquid glucose – 225 gms
Milk chocolate – 225 gms
Condensed milk – 160 gms
Neutral glaze – 90 gms

Topping
Chocolate coffee beans
Chocolate decorations for the sides

Almond dacquoise: Whip egg whites and caster sugar to a meringue. Fold in almond powder and icing sugar. Spread onto a parchment lined baking sheet and sprinkle with chopped almonds. Bake at 200°C in a preheated oven for 8-10 minutes. Cool and cut into 12 rounds of 6 cm each.

Coffee cream: Soften gelatin in 20 gms cold water. Boil milk, cream and roasted coffee beans. Let it infuse for about 30 minutes, re-boil and strain. Whip egg yolks and sugar until foamy, add warm coffee mixture and cook to 86°C. Add gelatin to the boiled mixture and allow it to cool to 28-29°C. Fold in the whipped cream.

In six silicone molds of 6 cm in diameter, put a disc of almond dacquoise. Divide the coffee cream into six portions and pour a portion on six of the dacquoise. Immediately cover with another dacquoise and press lightly. Freeze the assembled sandwiches.

Chocolate mouse: Soften gelatin powder in 50 gms cold water. Whip egg yolks and caster sugar well, add the boiled milk and cook to 86°C, stir in gelatin and pour over the already melted chocolate. Stir well until dissolved, cool to 35°C. Slowly fold in the whipped cream. Line 8 cm diameter rings with acetate strips. Pour some mousse at the bottom. Now place the frozen dacquoise and coffee cream sandwich. Cover with chocolate mousse. Level and freeze.

Milk chocolate glaze: Soften gelatin in 125 gms of cold water. Bring the water, sugar and glucose to a boil and cook to 103°C. Place the milk chocolate into a medium size bowl with softened gelatin. Pour the hot sugar-glucose mixture onto the chocolate and emulsify with a hand blender. Add the condensed milk and neutral glaze, stirring well. Again, mix well with hand blender. Cover with cling film and refrigerate overnight.

Remove the frozen cakes from the molds and place on a wire rack. Pour the milk chocolate glaze at 35°C from above to cover the top and sides. Decorate with chocolate coffee beans and chocolate decorations.

JUST A PINCH

MASALA CHAI CAKES

Yield – 6 treats

Salted caramel pate
Caster sugar – 150 gms
Liquid glucose – 110 gms
Isomalt – 110 gms
Cream 35% – 375 gms
Invert sugar – 25 gms
Unsalted butter – 15 gms
Seeds of 1 Vanilla bean
Fleur de sel – 2 gms
Melted Cocoa butter – 25 gms
Dark chocolate 60-70% – 75 gms

Cake
Unsalted butter, soft – 250 gms
Brown sugar – 220 gms
Honey – 80 gms
Eggs – 2
Baking powder – 1 tsp
Baking soda – ¼ tsp
Fleur de sel – ½ tsp
Cinnamon powder – 1 tbsp
Ginger powder – 2 tsp
Cardamom powder – 2 tsp
Allspice – 1½ tsp
Black pepper powder – ½ tsp
All-purpose flour – 280 gms
Yogurt – 250 gms
Vanilla extract – 2 tsp

Salted caramel pate: Heat cream, invert sugar, salt and vanilla seeds. Make a caramel with sugar, glucose and isomalt, then deglaze with butter and add cream mixture. Give one boil and pour over chocolate and cocoa butter. Mix with hand blender. Store in jars.

Cake: In a large bowl, beat together the butter, brown sugar, and honey until smooth and somewhat lighter in colour. Add the eggs one at a time. Stir in the baking powder, baking soda, salt and spices. Add flour and yogurt alternatively in two lots and fold.

Scoop the batter into the greased bundt molds and bake for 30 to 40 minutes until a skewer inserted in the centre comes out clean. Remove the cake from the oven, and cool in the pan for 15 minutes before turning it out onto a rack to finish cooling.

Sprinkle with icing sugar. Serve with salted caramel pate.

BOURBON BUNDLES

Yield – 15 treats

Brownies
Dark chocolate 60-70% – 240 gms
Unsalted butter – 135 gms
Eggs – 2
Brown sugar – 135 gms
Caster sugar – 100 gms
Bourbon – 80 ml
Vanilla extract – 2 tsp
All-purpose flour – 160 gms
Cocoa powder – 8 gms
Pecans, roughly chopped – 150 gms

Chocolate sauce
Caster sugar – 50 gms
Cream 35% – 300 gms
Dark chocolate 60-70% – 150 gms

Brownies: Line a 33 x 23 cm pan with parchment paper on sides and bottom and keep ready. Melt the chocolate with butter in microwave. Beat the eggs with both the sugars until it has almost dissolved and the mixture turns light and creamy. Add the melted chocolate and butter to the beaten eggs and sugar and continue to mix well, then add the bourbon and vanilla. After having sifted the flour and cocoa twice, beat this into the chocolate mixture. Finally fold the chopped pecans. Pour into the pan and bake at 180°C for 20 minutes or until a skewer inserted in the centre comes out clean. Cool on a wire rack. Cut into rectangular pieces.

Chocolate sauce: Tip the sugar into a small saucepan and melt over low heat. Add half tablespoon of water, and dissolve the sugar without stirring. Bring to boil and continue to cook the syrup until it becomes an amber-colored caramel. Remove the pan from the heat and slowly add the cream, stirring constantly to combine. Return the pan to a low heat to melt the hardened caramel that might have formed at the bottom of the pan. Once the caramel cream is smooth but not quite boiling, add the chocolate. Remove from the heat and stir gently until thoroughly combined. Cool to room temperature. Pour the chocolate sauce over the brownie pieces and decorate with roasted cocoa nibs and edible gold stars.

Mark
KENTUCKY STRAIGHT
HANDMADE
750ml. 45%alc./vol.

CINNAROUNDS

Yield – 20 treats

Doughnuts
All-purpose flour – 500 gms
Active dry yeast – 7 gms
Unsalted butter, melted and cooled – 100 gms
Caster sugar – 30 gms
Egg – 1
Ground nutmeg – 1 pinch
Ground allspice – 1 pinch
Milk, lukewarm – 250 ml
Fleur de sel – ½ tsp

Finishing
Peanut oil for deep frying
Cinnamon powder – 4 gms
Caster sugar – 250 gms

Traditionally, German doughnuts were fried in rendered animal fat called schmaltz.

Doughnuts: Put flour, yeast, butter, sugar, egg and spices into a mixing bowl. Add milk and salt and knead to a soft and smooth, non-sticking yeast dough. If required, add some flour to improve consistency. Cover and let it rest in a warm place until the dough has almost doubled its size.

Dust the workbench with flour and knead the risen dough to bring it together. Roll out the dough and cut with doughnut cutter. Transfer very carefully onto a parchment lined baking sheet. Cover this with a clean plastic sheet. Leave aside for about 30 minutes.

In a large wide pot, heat up the oil to 180°C. Very carefully slide in the doughnuts into the hot oil. Deep-fry them for about 2 minutes, and then flip them over and fry for another 2-3 minutes until golden brown.

Drain and cool the doughnuts down on kitchen paper, then roll in cinnamon and sugar mixed together.

CHOCOLATE MUD SLICES

Yield – 16 treats

Ganache
Cream – 300 gms
Dark chocolate 65-70% – 450 gms
Liquid glucose – 30 gms

Cake
Eggs – 6
Caster sugar – 300 gms
Unsalted butter – 300 gms
Dark chocolate 60-70% – 85 gms
All-purpose flour – 165 gms
Cocoa powder – 50 gms

Ganache: Boil cream and glucose in a heavy pan. Pour over chocolate. Leave for 5 minutes. Then stir in the centre to make an emulsion using a hand blender. Cover with cling film and leave to rest for at least two hours at room temperature.

Cake: Sift the flour and baking powder, set aside. Melt chocolate and butter together. Beat eggs and sugar in a stand mixer with whisk attachment till the sugar is dissolved but stop beating before it becomes light and fluffy. Fold in the melted chocolate and butter. Lastly fold in the sifted flour and cocoa lightly without removing any air from the batter. Pour into a greased and lined 25 x 25 cm square pan. Bake at 170°C in a preheated oven for about 20-25 minutes. Remove from oven and cool completely in the pan. Invert on a wire rack. Cover with ganache and cut into pieces.

RASPBERRY PATE DE FRUIT

Yield – 50 treats

Raspberry puree – 500 gms
Sugar – 570 gms
Liquid glucose – 100 gms
Citric acid – 8 gms
Yellow pectin – 10 gms

Rolling
Granulated sugar – 250 gms
Citric acid – 5 gms

Dilute citric acid in 8 gms water and keep ready. Mix about 50 gms of sugar with the pectin. Whisk together really well. Heat the raspberry puree to 50°C Add the pectin/sugar mixture all the while whisking the mixture. Bring to a boil for one minute. Add the glucose and the rest of the sugar. Cook mixture to 106°C. Then stir in the citric acid/water mixture. Cook for one more minute. Pour into a semi-sphere silicone mold or any other shape as desired. Cool for a few hours. Roll in granulated sugar mixed with citric acid.

SCANDI BARS

Yield – 24 treats

Crust
All-purpose flour – 280 gms
Icing sugar – 160 gms
Unsalted butter – 180 gms

Topping
Apricot preserves – 250 gms
Egg whites – 2
Icing sugar – 160 gms
Almond extract – 1 tsp
Almonds, sliced – 50 gms

Crust: Line the bottom of a 33 x 23 cm baking pan with aluminum foil, extending the foil over the long sides of the pan. Lightly spray the foil with nonstick cooking spray. Combine the flour and icing sugar for the crust in a large bowl. Add in the butter and mix with a pastry blender until mixture resembles coarse crumbs. Press into the baking pan, pressing about 1.5 cm up along the sides. Bake at 180°C in a preheated oven, for 15 to 20 minutes until the edges begin to lightly brown.

Topping: Beat the egg whites with a whisk until foamy. Beat in the icing sugar and almond extract. Spread the apricot preserve over the baked crust. Spoon the egg whites over the preserve. Sprinkle with the almonds. Bake again for 15 to 18 minutes or until the topping is golden brown. Run a metal spatula along the short sides of the pan to loosen the pastry. Using the foil, lift the pastry from the pan and cool completely on a wire rack then cut into squares.

ROSE BABAS

Yield – 12 treats

Babas
Instant dry yeast – 7 gms
Caster sugar (A) – ¼ tsp
Warm water – 30 ml
All-purpose flour – 250 gms
Fleur de sel – a pinch
Eggs – 2
Egg yolk – 1
Caster sugar (B) – 40 gms
Rose extract – ½ tsp
Vanilla extract – 1 tsp
Unsalted butter,
soft – 90 gms
Scented syrup (see right)
Greek yoghurt – 250 gms

Scented syrup
Water – 350 ml
Caster sugar – 250 gms
Rose water – 60 ml
Rose extract – ⅛ tsp

Decoration
Pink peppercorns
Rose petals
Raspberry juice

Babas: Stir together the yeast, the sugar (A), and the warm water in a cup. Allow the mixture to stand until swollen, 6-7 minutes. Put the flour and salt in the bowl of a stand mixer with paddle attachment. Separately whisk the whole eggs, egg yolk, sugar (B), the rose extract, and vanilla extract in a bowl. Blend in the yeast mixture. Pour the egg-yeast mixture over the sifted flour and stir to mix. Add the butter. Beat the dough on low speed until just combined, and then increase the speed to moderate and beat for 4 to 5 minutes longer, or until silky and smooth.

Turn the dough into a bowl heavily coated with softened unsalted butter, lightly turn dough to coat all sides in a film of butter, make several cuts in the dough with a pair of kitchen scissors. Cover tightly with cling film and leave at room temperature for an hour and a half to rise. Turn the dough out onto a work surface and divide it into 12 even-size pieces.

To form the babas, smooth each piece of dough into a plump ball by rolling it briskly on the work surface in the cupped palm of your hand. Place a ball of dough in each of the buttered molds; each mold should be filled no more than one-third by the ball of dough. Arrange the molds on the sheet pan. Cover the babas with cling film. Leave to rise at room temperature for 1 hour and 15 minutes or until just about tripled in bulk.

Leave the babas on the rimmed pan and bake at 180°C in a preheated oven for 15 to 18 minutes until set. Transfer the baba molds to cooling racks and let stand for 15 minutes. Carefully unmold the babas and continue to cool. Place the warm scented syrup in a large heatproof mixing bowl. Add the babas to the syrup, a few at a time, and let them soak up the syrup, turning and rolling them over and then place on a cooling rack. Serve the babas with softly whipped yoghurt and decorate with pink peppercorns and rose petals. Add a pipette containing rose water and some raspberry juice.

Scented syrup: Place the water and sugar in a medium-size saucepan, cover, and place over moderately low heat. When the sugar has dissolved, uncover the pan, raise the heat to high, and boil for 6 minutes. Add the rose water and simmer for 3 minutes. Remove the syrup from the heat and stir in the rose extract. Pour the syrup into a bowl and use lukewarm.

This recipe is a non-alcoholic version of the traditional preparation.

STRAWBERRY & CHEESE BRIOCHE

Yield – 12 treats

Cheese filling
Cream cheese – 200 gms
Icing sugar – 10 gms
Cornstarch – 10 gms
Seeds of ½ Vanilla bean

Streusel topping
Caster sugar – 75 gms
All-purpose flour – 170 gms
Unsalted butter, cold – 120 gms
Strawberries halved – 6

Brioche dough
Unsalted butter, chilled, cubed – 70 gms
Water – 50 gms
Egg – 1
Active dry yeast – 1 tsp
All-purpose flour – 250 gms
Caster sugar – 25 gms
Fleur de sel – ½ tsp

Egg wash
Egg – 1
Water – 1 tbsp
Fleur de sel – a pinch

Cheese filling: Mix the cream cheese, icing sugar, cornstarch, and vanilla seeds together in a medium bowl. Set the mixture aside.

Streusel topping: Mix all the ingredients till crumbly and spread on a baking sheet and refrigerate till ready for use.

Brioche dough: Add the flour, egg, sugar, salt, yeast and water in a bowl of a stand mixer with a dough hook and mix at low speed to combine the ingredients. Scrape the bottom and sides of the bowl occasionally. It should take about 2 minutes for the dough to come together.

Increase the speed to a medium and knead until smooth dough forms, about 4 minutes. You can add a little water if the dough is too stiff, or a little flour if it is too slack. Reduce the mixer speed to low and begin adding the butter, a little bit at a time.

Shape the dough into a ball, put in the bowl and cover with cling film and let it rise at room temperature until the dough has nearly doubled in volume, about one hour.

Place the brioche dough on a lightly floured work surface and divide it into 12 pieces. Form a nice ball with each piece. Place them on a parchment paper-lined sheet pan.

Egg wash: In a small bowl, whisk the egg, water, and salt together to make an egg wash. Brush each dough ball with some of the egg wash. Use fingers to press down in the middle of a ball to make a very deep impression. Spoon the cheese mixture in the deep impression. Top each bun with halved strawberries.

Cover the filled buns with a towel and set them aside to rise at room temperature for about 1 hour until a finger pressed into the side of a bun leaves only a slight depression. Brush again with egg wash and sprinkle streusel on the sides.

Bake this at 160°C in a preheated oven until golden brown, about eight minutes. Remove from the oven and set aside to cool on the sheet pan before serving, either warm or at room temperature.

BROWN THE BRIOCHE

Yield – 12 treats

Streusel
Caster sugar – 60 gms
Unsalted butter,
soft – 30 gms
Fleur de sel – a pinch
All-purpose flour – 30 gms
Hazelnut powder – 40 gms

Salted caramel pate
Caster sugar – 150 gms
Liquid glucose – 110 gms
Isomalt – 110 gms
Cream 35% – 375 gms
Invert sugar – 25 gms
Unsalted butter – 15 gms
Seeds of 1 Vanilla bean
Fleur de sel – 2 gms
Melted cocoa butter – 25 gms
Dark chocolate 60-70% –
75 gms

Brioche
All-purpose flour – 185 gms
Fleur de sel – 5 gms
Caster sugar – 20 gms
Eggs – 3
Instant dry yeast – 4 gms
Unsalted butter,
cubed – 150 gms
Egg yolks, well mixed – 2

Topping
Muscovado sugar

Streusel: Mix all the ingredients together until crumbly, and spread on a parchment lined tray and freeze.

Salted caramel pate: Heat cream, invert sugar, salt and vanilla seeds. Make a caramel with sugar, glucose and isomalt, then deglaze with butter and add cream mixture. Give one boil and pour over chocolate and cocoa butter. Mix with hand blender. Store in jars.

Brioche: Mix flour, salt, sugar and yeast in the bowl of a stand mixer. Add eggs gradually. Make a dough and knead till it is smooth. Add cubed butter bit by bit. Make sure the temperature of the cough does not exceed 22°C. Make a ball, put in a bowl and let it rise to double the volume at room temperature. Fold the dough to remove some of the air. Again put back in bowl and reserve in fridge for two hours. Once again, fold the dough and leave to rest overnight.

Next day, divide the dough into 12 pieces. Shape into balls and put in small molds. Brush the top with egg yolks. Let it rest till it doubles .Glaze again with egg yolks. Sprinkle streusel and Muscovado sugar. Bake at 180°C in a preheated oven for 15-20 minutes until golden. Serve with salted caramel pate.

CHOCOLATE MINI ME

Yield – 40 treats

Friands
Dark chocolate, 60-70% – 340 gms
Unsalted butter – 450 gms
Caster sugar – 620 gms
All-purpose flour – 210 gms
Cornstarch – 15 gms
Eggs – 8

Ganache
Dark chocolate, 60-70% – 230 gms
Cream, 35% – 300 gms

Topping
Almonds, blanched and sliced

Friands: Melt the butter over medium heat until hot. Pour the butter over the chocolate and whisk or stir until smooth. Combine the sugar, flour, cornstarch and salt and mix well. Add the flour mixture to the chocolate mixture in three batches, whisking well after each addition. Add eggs, one by one, and whisk until combined.

Pour the batter in small paper muffin cups, and bake at 180°C in a preheated oven for 12-15 minutes. Remove from oven and leave to cool.

Ganache: Bring the cream to just under a boil in a small saucepan. Pour the cream over the chocolate and let it sit for a minute or two. Stir gently with a rubber spatula until the chocolate is melted and smooth. Leave to rest for one hour. Pipe with a star tip on top of the baked friands. Decorate with a few almond slices.

NORMANDY BRIOCHES

Yield – 10 treats

Diced apple
Apples – 2
Calvados – ½ tsp
Fleur de sel – a pinch

Apple crisps
Apple – 1
Water – 500 ml
Sugar – 650 gms

Brioche dough
Strong flour – 500 gms
Fresh yeast – 15 gms
Water – 20 ml
Caster sugar – 60 gms
Salt – 10 gms
Eggs – 6
Vanilla extract – ½ tsp
Unsalted butter, soft and cubed – 250 gms

Topping
Egg, beaten –1
Apricot glaze

Diced apple: Peel the two apples and cut into cubes (approximately 300 gms). Add the Calvados and a pinch of salt. Mix all the ingredients together and keep aside in the refrigerator.

Apple crisps: Bring the water and sugar to a boil, cool. Slice 10 thin rings from the apple using a mandolin. Place the slices into the cold sugar syrup and refrigerate.

Brioche dough: Place the flour into a large bowl; make a well in the centre. Dissolve the yeast in the water and pour into the well. Sprinkle the sugar and salt onto the flour. Beat the eggs in a small bowl, pour ¾ into the well, add vanilla to the remaining egg and refrigerate. Mix the flour with the liquid ingredients to form a soft, moist but manageable dough.

Dust the work surface with flour and turn out the dough. Knead for approximately 10 minutes or until a smooth, elastic dough is formed. Flatten the dough lengthways with the palm of your hand and then dot the dough with small pieces softened butter and fold the dough over to enclose the butter. Knead until the butter is incorporated. The dough is well kneaded when it is smooth and elastic. Fold in the remaining vanilla-egg mixture. Shape into a ball and place the dough in a lightly floured clean bowl, cover with plastic wrap and refrigerate for 12 hours.

Turn the brioche dough onto a lightly floured work surface and knead for one minute to soften. Divide the dough into 10 balls and place on baking sheets. Transfer to the refrigerator and leave to rest for at least for 15 minutes. Return the balls of dough to the floured work surface and light roll each to form flat disks. Place equal amounts of diced apple in the centre of the disks of dough. Fold the edges into the centre and pinch to seal. The apple cubes should be enclosed in dough. Fill each piece snuggly into buttered pastry rings placed on a parchment lined baking sheet. Brush with egg wash. Leave to rise at room temperature for two hours or until doubled in size.

Brush the brioche dough again with egg wash. Drain the apple crisps and place one on top of each dough filled pastry ring, secure each slice with three wooden toothpicks. Bake at 200°C in preheated oven for 10 to 12 minutes, remove and cool.

Warm the apricot glaze over low heat. Brush the slices of apple crisp with apricot glaze.

TOFFEE APPLE TOWERS

Yield – 12 treats

Cupcakes
Unsalted butter, soft – 60 gms
All-purpose flour – 150 gms
Baking powder – ½ tsp
Ground cinnamon – 1 tsp
Brown sugar – 110 gms
Maple syrup – 80 gms
Eggs – 2
Pecans, chopped – 80 gms
Apple, grated – 85 gms

Maple frosting
Unsalted butter, soft – 90 gms
Icing sugar – 160 gms
Maple syrup – 2 tsp

Decoration
Isomalt – 150 gms
Pecans, chopped – 50 gms
Pink peppercorns – 10 gms

Cupcakes: Line 12-hole standard muffin pan with paper cases. Beat butter, flour, baking powder, cinnamon, sugar, syrup and eggs in a bowl of a stand mixer fitted with paddle attachment on low speed until ingredients are combined. Increase speed to medium; beat until mixture changes to a pale colour. Stir in nuts and grated apple. Divide mixture among cases; smooth the tops. Bake batter at 160°C in a preheated oven, for about 25 minutes. Turn cakes onto wire rack to cool.

Maple frosting: Beat butter, sifted icing sugar and syrup in small bowl of a stand mixer until light and fluffy and ready to pipe.

Decoration: Spread isomalt on a silicone mat. Sprinkle pecans and peppercorns and cover with another silicone mat. Bake at 200°C in a preheated oven for about 10-15 minutes till isomalt is melted. Cool and cut into shards for decoration.

Pipe cakes with frosting with spaghetti tip; decorate with isomalt shards.

ORANGE IN THE MIDDLE CAKES

Yield – 12 treats

Orange marmalade
Oranges – 2
Water – 850 ml
Caster sugar – 500 gms

Chocolate cake
Unsalted butter, soft – 360 gms
Caster sugar – 450 gms
Pure vanilla extract – 1 tbsp
Eggs, room temperature – 3
All-purpose flour – 210 gms
Baking soda – 1 tsp
Fleur de sel – ½ tsp
Water, hot – 150 ml
Cocoa powder – 65 gms
Instant coffee powder – 1 tsp
Cream 35% – 150 gms

Mocha frosting
Chocolate 60-70% – 360 gms
Unsalted butter, cubed – 45 gms
Instant coffee powder – 2 tsp
Cream 35% – 300 gms
Kahlúa – 1 tbsp
Vanilla extract – 1 tsp

Orange marmalade: Halve the oranges and squeeze the juice into a large stainless-steel pan. Scoop the pips and pulp into a sieve over the pan and squeeze out as much juice as possible, then tie the pulp and pips in the muslin. Shred the remaining peel and pith in a food processor. Add the shredded peel and muslin bag to the pan with the juice along with the water. Leave to soak overnight. This helps extract the maximum amount of pectin from the fruit pulp, which will give a better set.

Put the pan over a medium heat then bring up to a simmer. Cook uncovered, for 1½-2 hours, until the peels have become very soft. Carefully remove the muslin bag and allow to cool slightly. Squeeze out as much liquid as possible from the bag so as to extract the pectin. Discard the bag and weigh the softened peel mixture. This should be around 350–400 gms; if less, then top up with water to weigh 380 gms.

Add the sugar to the orange mixture, and put over a low heat. Warm gently so that the sugar dissolves completely, stirring occasionally. Do not boil before the sugar is dissolved. Increase the heat and bring up to the boil but do not stir while the marmalade is boiling. After about 5 minutes the marmalade will start to rise up in the pan (it may drop back and then rise again) and large bubbles will cover the surface. Cook to 105°C. Keep aside to cool.

Chocolate cake: Grease a 33 x 23 cm baking pan. Line with parchment paper. Place the butter and sugar in the bowl of a stand mixer fitted with the paddle attachment and beat on medium speed for 4 to 5 minutes until light and fluffy, occasionally scraping down the bowl. Add the vanilla, then beat in the eggs, one at a time on medium speed till well mixed and the batter is smooth.

Sift the flour, baking soda, and salt together in a medium bowl. In another bowl, whisk together the hot water, cocoa powder, and coffee powder until smooth. Add the cream and continue to whisk until smooth. With the mixer on low speed, add flour and chocolate mixtures alternately. (The flour to be added in three batches, and the chocolate mixture in two batches.) With a rubber spatula, scrape down the bowl to be sure the all the batter is well mixed. Pour the batter into the prepared pan, smooth the top, and bake for 25 to 35 minutes, until a skewer inserted in the centre comes out clean. Cool completely in the pan. Turn out onto a flat board. Put a layer of orange marmalade and frost the top with the mocha frosting as given below.

Mocha frosting: Place the chocolate, butter, and coffee powder in a bowl. Heat the cream on simmer and then pour it over the chocolate mixture, stirring occasionally, until the chocolate is melted. Stir in the Kahlúa and vanilla and stir until the mixture is smooth. Cover and refrigerate for 30 minutes until cool but not cold.

Place the cool mixture in a bowl of a stand mixer and beat on high speed for 15 to 20 seconds, not more, until the mixture forms soft peaks. Spread the frosting over the marmalade immediately with the metal spatula. Freeze and then cut into 12 rectangles. Sprinkle with cocoa powder and chocolate decorations.

COOKIE CAKES

Yield – 12 treats

Cookies
Dark chocolate, 60-70%, chopped – 60 gms
Milk chocolate, chopped – 60 gms
Unsalted butter – 85 gms
All-purpose flour – 90 gms
Egg – 1
Baking powder – 4 gms
Pecans, chopped – 130 gms

Madeleines
Caster sugar – 140 gms
Honey – 20 gms
Eggs – 3
All-purpose flour – 150 gms
Baking powder – 5 gms
Unsalted butter, melted – 140 gms
Zest of 1 lemon

Cookies: Sift flour and baking powder and keep aside. Mix butter and brown sugar and stir until it starts to turn pale. Incorporate the egg, then the sifted flour. Add the milk and dark chocolate and chopped pecans. Roll into sausage shape and cover in cling film, and store in the freezer.

Madeleines: Sift flour and baking powder and keep aside. Mix the honey into the eggs, followed by sugar, zest and sifted flour. Leave the mix to rest in the refrigerator for two hours.

Assembly: Remove cookie dough from freezer and cut into 2-3 cm rounds. Place the rounds in a circular silicone mold. Bake at 160°C, in a preheated oven, for approximately seven minutes. Take the dough out of the oven and pipe the madeleine mix onto the part-baked cookies. Bake again at 190°C for approximately seven minutes. Take out of the oven and leave to cool. Dust with icing sugar.

CHIPWICH BARS

Yield – 16 treats

Cookie layer
Unsalted butter, soft – 250 gms
Brown sugar – 75 gms
Egg – 1
Vanilla extract – 1 tsp
All-purpose flour – 300 gms
Fleur de sel – ½ tsp
Pecans, finely chopped – 100 gms

Topping
Liquid glucose – 200 gms
Brown sugar – 110 gms
Eggs – 2
Unsalted butter, melted – 30 gms
Vanilla extract – 1 tsp
Fleur de sel – ¼ tsp
Pecans, finely chopped – 150 gms
Dark chocolate chips – 350 gms

Cookie layer: Beat the butter and sugar in the bowl of a stand mixer with paddle attachment until light and fluffy. Add the egg and vanilla, and mix well. Reduce mixer speed to low. Gradually add the flour, pecans, and salt. Mix just until combined. Transfer the mixture to a greased and parchment lined 20 cm square pan, and press down evenly into the pan.

Bake at 180°C in a preheated oven, for 15 to 20 minutes until the edges are lightly browned. Set aside to cool slightly.

Topping: Combine the glucose, brown sugar, eggs, butter, vanilla, and salt until thoroughly mixed. Stir in the pecans. Pour the topping mixture over the cookie layer. Bake again for 35 to 40 minutes, or until the topping is set. Remove the pan from the oven and place on a wire rack.

Sprinkle the chocolate chips over the pecan topping. Let the chips sit for about five minutes. Spread lightly. Cool completely before cutting into bars.

ROLL IN THE ALPS

Yield – A 35 cm log

Strawberry confit
Strawberries,
quartered – 180 gms
Caster sugar – 110 gms
Lime juice – 10 gms
Lemon juice – 50 gms
NH Pectin – 25 gms

Lime whipped cream
Cream 35% – 150 gms
Icing sugar – 15 gms
Zest of 1 lime

Choux pastry
Milk – 70 gms
Water – 70 gms
Unsalted butter – 60 gms
Fleur de sel – a pinch
Caster sugar – 4 gms
Rice flour – 30 gms
All-purpose flour – 50 gms
Eggs – 3

Sponge biscuit
Choux pastry – 295 gms
Vegetable oil – 35 gms
Zest of ½ a lime
Egg whites – 3
Caster sugar – 60 gms

Vanilla butter cream
Water – 15 gms
Egg white – 1
Caster sugar – 60 gms
Unsalted butter,
soft – 100 gms
Seeds of 1 Vanilla bean

Strawberry confit: Mix the strawberries, caster sugar, lime juice and lemon juice in a bowl. Cover with cling film and macerate for 30 minutes. In a saucepan, warm the macerated strawberries with the maceration juice to 40°C. Add the pectin then bring to a boil for 30 seconds before removing the pan from the heat. Pour the confit of strawberries into a bowl, let it cool to room temperature, cover with cling f lm and keep in refrigerator.

Lime whipped cream: Whisk the cream with the icing sugar and lime zest. Store in the refrigerator till required.

Choux pastry: Bring the milk, water, butter, salt and sugar to a boil. Turn off the heat; add the sifted all-purpose flour and rice flour all at once. Using a spatula, mix for about one minute while still hot. Put it in the bowl of a stand mixer with whisk attachment and cool at medium speed. As soon as there is no steam escaping, incorporate the eggs one by one.

Sponge biscuit: Mix the prepared choux pastry, the oil, half of the caster sugar and the lime zest. Whisk the egg whites with the second half of the sugar and fold carefully in the choux pastry. Spread the batter on the parchment lined 35 x 25 cm baking sheet with 1 cm height and bake at 170°C in a preheated oven for 12 minutes.

Remove the biscuit from the baking sheet, while leaving it on the parchment paper. Let it cool to room temperature. Once cooled, place a second sheet of parchment over the biscuit, and then flip it over, before peeling off the original parchment.

Vanilla butter cream: In a saucepan, cook the sugar and water at 121°C. In a mixer, as soon as the thermometer reads 112°C, start to whisk the egg white at slow-medium speed. When the syrup is at 121°C, pour it on the egg white and increase the speed of the mixer. When the meringue is lukewarm gradually add the butter and vanilla seeds and whisk again till well incorporated.

Assembly: Spread a thin layer of strawberry confit on the entire surface of the sponge biscuit except on one side of the length where a 1 cm strip of biscuit is left without strawberry confit. Spread the lime whipped cream over the entire length of the biscuit, except for a strip 3 cm away from the edge on the opposite side of the 1 cm strip. Then roll the biscuit on itself, using parchment paper and making sure to tighten the biscuit around the lime whipped cream. Once well rolled up, place the rolled biscuit in the refrigerator for 30 minutes.

Place the butter cream in a piping bag with a star tip and pipe three strips lengthwise in the centre of the ready roll. Decorate as desired.

ROLL IN THE ALPS

ORANGE BROWNIES

Yield – 20 treats

Brownie
Semi-candied orange cubed – 75 gms
All-purpose flour – 70 gms
Cocoa powder – 8 gms
Unsalted butter, soft – 150 gms
Muscovado sugar – 75 gms
Caster sugar – 100 gms
Fleur de sel – 3 gms
Dark chocolate 60-70%, melted – 90 gms
Eggs – 2
Pecans, lightly toasted – 75 gms

Cocoa caviar
Water – 250 gms
Caster sugar – 50 gms
Agar agar – 2 gms
Cocoa powder – 30 gms
Sunflower oil – 1 litre

Chocolate covering
Dark chocolate 60-70% – 500 gms
Grapeseed oil – 50 ml

Ganache
Dark chocolate 60-70% – 250 gms
Cream 35% – 250 gms
Cointreau – 50 ml

Brownie: Sift the flour and cocoa powder and keep aside. In the bowl of an electric stand mixer, combine the butter, sugars, and salt; using the paddle attachment cream the mixture until lightened. Add the melted chocolate and mix. Add the egg and mix again. Add the sifted flour and mix just until combined. Fold in the pecans and the semi-candied orange. Transfer the mixture to a greased rectangular pan, spreading to fill the pan evenly. Bake brownie at 180°C in a preheated oven for 20-25 minutes. Remove from the oven and cool completely. Cut into 20 rectangles. Freeze.

Cocoa caviar: Combine all the ingredients except the sunflower oil. Bring to a boil while continuously stirring to prevent the cocoa from sticking to the bottom of the saucepan. Leave this to cool to 70°C.

Separately, half fill a rectangular container (approximately 7 cm high) with the oil at 6°C. Fill a syringe with the cocoa base and drip the mix into the oil. Allow the caviar drops to gel and settle on the bottom of the container before pouring new drops. Take out the caviar drops and rinse in warm water.

Chocolate covering: Chop the chocolate and melt slowly in the microwave at low power, stirring from time to time. Stir in the oil. Insert a knife in the frozen brownie to lift and dip in the icing. Remove the knife and keep chocolate covered brownie on a silicone mat.

Ganache: Heat the cream until simmering and pour over the chocolate. Stir until smooth and add the Cointreau. Set the ganache aside till it's ready to be piped.

Pipe on top of the chocolate covered brownie. Put some cocoa caviar on one side and garnish with chocolate decorations.

PINEAPPLE HIBISCUS CAKES

Yield – 12 treats

Pineapple cake
Vegetable oil – 125 ml
Eggs – 3
All-purpose flour – 225 gms
Caster sugar – 165 gms
Ground cinnamon – ½ tsp
Baking powder – ½ tsp
Carrot, coarsely grated – 440 gms
Pineapple, crushed and drained – 160 gms

Pineapple flowers
Caster sugar – 1 tbsp
Water – 1 tbsp
Fresh pineapple, wafer thin slices – 12

Lemon frosting
Unsalted butter, soft – 30 gms
Cream cheese, soft – 80 gms
Lemon rind, finely grated – 1 tsp
Icing sugar – 240 gms

Topping
Hibiscus flowers, stewed

Pineapple cake: Line a 12-hole standard muffin pan with paper cases. Combine oil, eggs, flour, baking powder, sugar and cinnamon in medium bowl; stir until combined. Stir in carrot and pineapple. Divide mixture among cases. Bake the cakes at 160°C in a preheated oven for about 30 minutes. Turn onto wire rack to cool.

Pineapple flowers: Stir sugar and the water together in a small saucepan over low heat until sugar has dissolved. Brush both sides of pineapple slices with sugar syrup. Place slices in a single layer on wire racks over oven trays. Dry sweetened pineapple slices at 120°C in oven for about one hour. Immediately remove slices from rack and carefully shape into flowers.

Lemon cream cheese frosting: Beat butter, cream cheese and rind in small bowl with electric mixer until light and fluffy; gradually beat in sifted icing sugar.

Spread or pipe lemon frosting on top of cakes. Decorate with pineapple flowers and stewed hibiscus flowers.

CANDY CRUNCH CUPCAKES

Yield – 12 treats

Cupcakes
All-purpose flour – 350 gms
Baking powder – 2 tsp
Fleur de sel – ¼ tsp
Unsalted butter, soft – 185 gms
Caster sugar – 300 gms
Eggs – 2
Egg yolks – 2
Vanilla extract – 2 tsp
Milk – 200 ml

Butter cream frosting
Unsalted butter, soft – 125 gms
Icing sugar, sifted – 700 gms
Vanilla extract – 2 tsp
Cream, 35% – 100 gms
Caramel colour – as required

Popcorn croquant
Popcorn kernels, air-popped – 50 gms
Caster sugar – 400 gms
Liquid glucose – 75 gms
Water – 175 ml
Unsalted butter, cubed – 125 gms
Fleur de sel – ¼ tsp
Baking soda – ½ tsp
Vanilla extract – 2 tsp

Cupcake: Sift the flour, baking powder, and salt and keep aside. Cream the butter in the large bowl of a stand mixer with paddle attachment on moderately high speed for three minutes. Add the sugar and beat again. Beat in the eggs, one at a time, and then blend in the egg yolks and vanilla extract. On low speed, in alternative batches add the sifted flour and milk.

Spoon the batter into greased ring molds, dividing it evenly among them. It should not be filled more than two-third. Bake at 180°C in the preheated oven for 20 minutes, or until a skewer comes clean when inserted into the cake.

Cool the cakes in the pans on racks for 10 minutes, then remove them from the pan to wire cooling racks.

Butter cream frosting: Place the butter in the bowl of a stand mixer with the paddle attachment. Beat on moderate speed for one minute. Add about half of the icing sugar, vanilla extract, and the cream. Beat for one minute on moderately low speed. Add the remaining icing sugar and beat until smooth. The smoothness of the frosting can be adjusted by adding either more cream or icing sugar. Mix in the colour and beat for 45 seconds to one minute on low speed to integrate the colour. Use the frosting immediately.

Popcorn croquant: Heat sugar, glucose, water and butter in a saucepan. Cook to 145°C. Remove from heat and add in salt, baking soda and vanilla. Pour over the popcorn, which is in a large mixing bowl, and stir to coat it well. Spread on a baking sheet as quickly as possible. Cool before breaking it into small clusters. Store in airtight container.

Assembly: Pipe the frosting with a star tip, on the top and sides of the cupcakes. Decorate with popcorn croquants.

Any nut can replace the popcorn for the croquant recipe.

CHOCOLATE MANGO MELODY

Yield – 6 treats

Coffee sablé
All-purpose flour – 250 gms
Unsalted butter – 150 gms
Icing sugar – 100 gms
Egg – 1
Baking powder – ¼ tsp
Instant coffee – 8 gms

Crispy hazelnut praline
Milk chocolate, melted – 35 gms
Unsalted butter, melted – 25 gms
Hazelnut praline – 145 gms
Paillete Feuilletine – 60 gms

Mango & chocolate mousse
Mango puree – 215 gms
Milk chocolate, melted – 340 gms
Cream 35%, softly whipped – 400 gms
Gelatin powder – 6 gms

Chocolate glaze
Cream 35% – 300 gms
Water – 100 gms
Sugar – 90 gms
NH pectin – 2 gms
Liquid glucose – 110 gms
Milk chocolate – 700 gms
Gelatin powder – 10 gms

Coffee sable: Mix flour, baking powder, coffee and icing sugar together. Add butter and mix till crumbly. Add egg and make a homogenous mixture. Make a ball and cover with cling film. Refrigerate for a few hours. Roll out to 5 mm thickness and cut into rounds that are a little smaller than the mold/molds to be used.

Crispy hazelnut praline: Combine the chocolate and butter; add the hazelnut praline and finally the feuilletine. Once again, prepare thin cisks that are the same size as the sable. Store in freezer and keep ready to insert into the cake.

Mango & chocolate mousse: Soften gelatin in 30 gms cold water. Separately, heat half the mango puree and dissolve the gelatin in it. Add in the rest of the puree. Mix with the chocolate and emulsify with hand blender. At 35°C, add in the whipped cream. Line the molds with acetate. Pour a bit of mousse and insert the frozen crispy praline, pour some more mousse and then cover with coffee sable. Freeze.

Chocolate glaze: Soften gelatin in 50 gms cold water. Heat the cream and the water, and when at 40°C, sprinkle in the mixture of sugar and pectin. Add in the glucose and bring to a boil. Remove from heat and add softened gelatin. Pour over the milk chocolate at intervals in order to emulsify. Strain and store in refrigerator. Use at 30°C. Glaze the frozen cakes and garnish with chocolate decorations and fresh mango scooped out in balls.

CHOCBLOCS

Yield – 16 treats

Praline cake
Almond praline – 285 gms
Invert sugar – 25 gms
Eggs – 4
Fleur de sel – 3.5 gms
Vegetable oil – 80 gms
All-purpose flour – 110 gms
Baking powder – 5 gms

Crumble
Unsalted butter, cubed – 80 gms
Brown sugar – 100 gms
All-purpose flour – 90 gms
Ground coffee – 10 gms
Instant coffee – 3 gms
Fleur de sel – a pinch
Milk chocolate, melted – 40 gms
Almonds, roasted, chopped – 25 gms
Cocoa butter, melted – 5 gms
Unsalted butter, melted – 10 gms
Almond praline – 20 gms

Praline glaze
Almond praline – 125 gms
Milk chocolate, melted – 375 gms
Cocoa butter, melted – 375 gms
Unsalted butter, melted – 75 gms

Orange confit
Orange rind, cut in large pieces – 50 gms
Orange juice – 150 gms
Caster sugar – 75 gms

Praline cake: Sift flour and baking powder and keep aside. Mix praline and invert sugar in a bowl of stand of a stand mixer with paddle attachment. Mix in the eggs one by one. Add salt and oil and mix. Fold in the flour. Bake in a greased and parchment lined 23 cm square tin till a skewer inserted in the centre comes out clean. Cool on a wire rack.

Crumble: Put butter, sugar, flour, coffee and salt in mixer and blend. Make it a crumble and spread on a baking sheet and bake at 160°C in a preheated oven for about 10 minutes till golden brown. Cool and mix 130 gms of the crumble with melted chocolate, coco butter, butter, praline and roasted almonds. Keeping aside some for decoration, spread the rest on the 23 cm square tin to a height of 5-mm. Cool in refrigerator till set.

Praline glaze: Mix all the ingredients and use at 23°C.

Orange confit: Put the orange rind in a saucepan. Cover with water and bring to a boil. Drain and again repeat the process twice. Put the drained and cooked orange rind with juice and sugar in a heavy-duty saucepan and cook on medium heat for 40-50 minutes. When sufficiently reduced and a little juice remains, blend in a food processor. Use sparingly as it is very intense and concentrated.

Assembly: Spread the orange confit on the crumble and cover with the praline cake. Freeze the assembly. Lightly on the frozen crumble insert a knife into the cut pieces and use as a stick to immerse into the glaze, making sure the coating is even all around. Decorate with orange confit pieces and crumble before the glaze sets.

Invert sugar helps to keep the cake super moist.

CHOCOLATE COSMOS

Yield – 10 treats

Orange confit
Oranges – 170 gms
Water – 750 gms
Salt – 2 gms
Orange puree – 25 gms
Lemon puree – 100 gms
Pectin NH – 3 gms
Caster sugar – 110 gms

Chocolate cake
Egg whites – 4
Caster sugar – 80 gms
Egg – 1
Egg yolks – 5
Invert sugar – 30 gms
All-purpose flour – 25 gms
Cacao powder – 15 gms
Ground almonds – 40 gms
Olive oil – 20 gms

Chocolate pastry cream
Corn starch – 20 gms
Milk – 250 gms
Cream 35% – 75 gms
Caster sugar (A) – 30 gms
Seeds of 1 Vanilla bean
Egg yolks – 2
Caster sugar (B) – 20 gms
Gelatin powder – 4 gms
Dark chocolate 60-70% – 75 gms

Chocolate diplomat cream
Chocolate pastry cream – 250 gms (recipe on right)
Cream 35%, whipped – 75 gms

Chocolate crumble
Unsalted butter – 75 gms
Brown sugar – 90 gms
Fleur de sel – a pinch
All-purpose flour – 70 gms
Polenta – 30 gms
Cacao powder – 15 gms
Almond powder – 40 gms

Chocolate crumble
Unsalted butter – 75 gms
Brown sugar – 90 gms
Fleur de sel – a pinch
All-purpose flour – 70 gms
Polenta – 30 gms
Cacao powder – 15 gms
Almond powder – 40 gms

Orange confit: Wash the oranges and cut into thin slices. Remove the seeds and white pith of the oranges. Bring the water and salt to a boil. Blanch the oranges for three minutes, sieve and rinse with cold water. Mix the pectin and sugar. Heat the orange and lemon puree, and then add the pectin. Add the oranges pieces and cook all for approx. 15-20 minutes to obtain a soft confit. Chop finely or puree. Refrigerate.

Chocolate cake: Whisk the egg whites and sugar to obtain a meringue. In a separate bowl whip the whole egg, egg yolks and invert sugar to obtain a creamy white mass. Incorporate the egg-mixture into the meringue. Sieve the flour and cacao powder and mix with the ground almonds. Carefully incorporate into the egg-mixture. Finally, add the olive oil. Spread the batter onto a parchment lined baking tray. Bake at 170°C in a preheated oven for 12 minutes. After baking, immediately turn over and place onto a wire rack to cool.

Chocolate pastry cream: Soften gelatin in 20 gms cold water. Dissolve the cornstarch with some of the cold milk. Boil the remaining milk, cream, sugar (A) and vanilla. Combine the egg yolks, the sugar (B) and dissolved corn starch and whip to obtain a creamy white mixture. Add the hot liquid to the egg yolk mixture and bring to a boil. Add the softened gelatin. Fold in the chocolate and stir thoroughly. Pour onto a tray covered with plastic film. Cover with another plastic film and refrigerate immediately.

Chocolate diplomat cream: Stir the pastry cream to obtain a smooth mass. In two batches delicately fold in the whipped cream. Place the cream in the refrigerator

Chocolate crumble: Cream the butter, brown sugar and salt together. Mix all the remaining ingredients and mix. Knead for a very short time to make crumbly dough. Refrigerate first and then bake at 140°C in a preheated oven for about 20 minutes

Caramelised hazelnuts: Make syrup with water and sugar. Bring to a boil. Add hazelnuts and simmer for a few minutes, drain and roast in oven at 160°C in a preheated oven for 20 minutes. Add cocoa butter. Separate and leave to cool on a silicone mat.

Assembly: Using a cutter, slice the cake and place it inside the ring. Pipe some orange confit on top of the sponge, spread with a spatula. Pipe some chocolate diplomat cream and put pieces of chocolate crumble. Decorate with caramelised hazelnuts and chocolate rings.

KICKSTART GRANOLA

Yield – 600 gms

Granola
Rolled oats – 200 gms
Red quinoa – 60 gms
Hazelnuts, chopped – 100 gms
Cinnamon, ground – ½ tsp
Fleur de sel – a pinch
Coconut oil, melted – 60 gms
Unsalted butter, soft – 60 gms
Maple syrup – 125 gms
Vanilla extract – 1 tsp
Dried cherries, roughly chopped – 60 gms

Chocolate coconut bites
Dark chocolate 60-70%, melted – 65 gms
Coconut flakes, unsweetened – 25 gms
Chia seeds – 5 gms

Granola: In a large mixing bowl, stir together the oats, quinoa, chopped hazelnuts, cinnamon and salt. In a separate bowl, whisk together the melted coconut oil, butter, honey and vanilla until uniform. Pour the liquid ingredients over the oat mixture and stir until evenly coated. Spread out evenly on a baking sheet and bake in a preheated oven at 170°C for 20-25 minutes or until golden and fragrant. Cool completely before storing. Mix in dried cherries.

Chocolate coconut bites: Stir together the melted chocolate, coconut flakes, and chia seeds. Using an offset spatula spread onto a sheet of parchment paper. Place in the freezer for about 10-15 minutes until solidified. Chop into rough pieces. Mix in to the cooled granola.

TOFFEE TUMBLES

Yield – 12 treats

Choux pastry
Unsalted butter – 60 gms
Water – 180 ml
All-purpose flour – 105 gms
Eggs – 3

Vanilla custard
Milk – 310 ml
Seeds of 1 Vanilla bean
Egg yolks – 4
Caster sugar – 110 gms
Cornflour – 40 gms

Almond buttercake
Unsalted butter,
soft – 150 gms
Almond essence – ½ tsp
Caster sugar – 150 gms
Eggs – 2
All-purpose flour – 125 gms
Baking powder – ½ tsp
Almond flour – 60 gms

Toffee
Caster sugar – 220 gms
Water – 125 ml

Choux pastry: Combine butter with water in medium saucepan; bring to a boil. Add flour, beat with wooden spoon over heat until mixture forms a smooth ball. Transfer mixture to small bowl; beat in eggs with electric mixer in about 6 batches until mixture becomes glossy. Spoon mixture into piping bag fitted with 1 cm plain tube. Pipe about 300 tiny drops of pastry (about ¼ level teaspoon) 2 cm apart, onto parchment lined trays. Bake pastry at 200°C in a preheated oven for 7 minutes. Reduce oven to 180°C, bake for another 5 minutes or until puffs are crisp.

Vanilla custard: Bring milk and vanilla seeds to a boil in small saucepan. Meanwhile, beat egg yolks, sugar and corn flour in small bowl with electric mixer until thick. Gradually beat in warm milk. Return custard to same pan; stir over heat until mixture boils and thickens. Cover surface of custard with plastic wrap. Cool in refrigerator.

Almond buttercake: Line 12-hole standard pan with paper cases. Beat butter, essence, sugar and eggs in small bowl with electric mixer until light and fluffy. Stir in sifted flour with baking powder and almond flour in two batches. Divide mixture among cases; smooth the surface to level. Bake cakes at 160°C in a preheated oven for about 20 minutes. Turn cakes onto wire rack to cool.

Toffee: Combine sugar with the water in small heavy-based saucepan. Stir over heat, without boiling, until sugar dissolves; bring to a boil. Reduce heat; simmer, uncovered, without stirring until mixture is golden brown. Remove from heat; let it stand until bubbles subside before using.

Assembly: Cut a 2 cm deep hole in the centre of each cake, fill with custard; replace lid. Spread tops of cakes with a little more custard. Top with a layer of puffs (choux pastry). Stack remaining puffs on cakes after dipping each in a little custard. Drizzle toffee over puffs.

NUTTY BLONDE CAKES

Yield – 20 treats

Cake
Cream, 35% – 185 gms
Caster sugar – 155 gms
Unsalted butter – 70 gms
Fleur de sel – a pinch
Brown sugar – 45 gms
Liquid glucose – 25 gms
Almond powder – 40 gms
Egg – 2
All-purpose flour – 75 gms
Baking powder – ½ tsp
Almonds, blanched, chopped – 100 gms

Caramel glaze
Water – 50 gms
Caster sugar – 50 gms
Neutral nappage – 200 gms

Cake: Boil cream and keep aside. Make a caramel by adding sugar gradually in a pan. Deglaze with hot cream and give it a boil. Pour in an airtight container and cool in refrigerator. Sieve flour, salt and baking powder and keep ready. Mix butter, brown sugar, glucose and almond powder in the bowl of a stand mixer with the paddle attachment. Add egg and then sifted flour. Mix till homogenized. Add the caramel.

Pipe in to small greased molds, of any desired shape. Sprinkle with almonds on top. Bake at 170°C in a preheated oven for 15-20 minutes. Cool on a wire rack.

Caramel glaze: Heat sugar and water in a heavy duty pan and make a caramel. Cool in refrigerator and mix with neutral nappage. Brush on top of piped cakes.

TROPICAL MOUSSE TARTS

Yield – 12 treats

Crust
Unsalted butter, soft – 100 gms
Caster sugar – 50 gms
All-purpose flour – 150 gms
Coconut, dried, shredded – 70 gms
Fleur de sel – a pinch

Mousse
Mangoes, puréed – 375 gms
Coconut cream – 115 gms
Fleur de sel – a pinch
Gelatin powder – 7 gms
Cream, 35%, softly whipped – 300 gms
Egg whites – 3
Caster sugar – 50 gms

Topping
Coconut shavings, fresh or toasted
Basil leaves
Mango, scooped

Crust: Mix the butter and sugar in the bowl of a stand mixer with paddle attachment, and beat until light. Add the flour and mix until it begins to hold together. Add the coconut and salt and mix gently until combined and crumbly. Gather into a ball. Cover with cling film. Chill in refrigerator until completely firm.

Remove the dough from the refrigerator and unwrap. Grate the dough evenly into a 23 x 33 cm baking dish by using the large holes of a box grater. The dough will be crumbly. Spread dough evenly on to the bottom of the dish, making sure the surface is covered, but do not press on it. Bake this at 160°C in a preheated oven until golden brown, about 20 minutes. Cool to room temperature.

Mousse: Soften gelatin in 35 gms cold water. Put the purée into a small saucepan and stir in the coconut cream and salt. Add gelatin and heat till gelatin is dissolved. Set aside to cool to room temperature. Put the egg whites and sugar into the bowl of a stand mixer. Set the bowl with the whites over the bain-marie, making sure the bottom of the bowl does not touch and the sugar is completely dissolved, about five minutes. Transfer bowl to the mixer, attach the whisk, and whip on medium-high for about five minutes, until the mixture holds medium-firm peaks but is still slightly warm.

With the mixer on low speed, add the cooled mango purée in a slow, steady stream and mix until just combined. Do not over-mix or the meringue will be deflated and the dessert will be too dense. Transfer the mango meringue to a large mixing bowl. Fold about half of cream into the meringue to lighten. Gently fold the remaining cream into the mango mixture, folding while turning the bowl, until the mixture is even and no streaks of meringue remain. Pour the mixture over the cooled crust and spread it gently and evenly with a small offset spatula. Chill until set, at least for about four hours or preferably overnight.

To serve, garnish with freshly scooped mango balls, coconut strips and a few leaves of fresh basil.

MATCHA SURPRISE

Yield – 12 Treats

Cake
Eggs – 5
Egg yolks – 3
Caster sugar – 140 gms
All-purpose flour – 40 gms
Cornflour – 10 gms
Matcha tea – 20 gms
Milk – 20 ml
Unsalted butter, melted – 20 gms
Egg whites – 4
Caster sugar – 50 gms

Praline Lemon
Caster sugar – 100 gms
Sorbitol powder – 5 gms
Water – 40 gms
Almonds – 175 gms
Lemon oil – a few drops

Praline Cream
Cream, 35% – 185 gms
Egg yolks – 2
Caster sugar – 25 gms
Praline lemon – 50 gms
(recipe on right)
Gelatin powder – 2 gms

Blackberry Cream
Cream, 35% – 110 gms
Egg yolks – 2
Caster sugar – 15 gms
Blackberry puree,
warmed – 145 gms
Dark chocolate, 60-70% –
120 gms
Invert sugar – 30 gms

Topping
Almonds, gold powder
coated
Matcha powder
Small meringues

Cake: Sieve flour, cornflour and matcha powder and set aside. Warm the eggs, egg yolks and sugar in the bowl of a stand mixer on a bain-marie. Return bowl to stand mixer and whip using the whisk attachment till light and fluffy and cool to touch. Mix melted butter and milk and blend with the sugar-egg mixture. Simultaneously, make a meringue with egg whites and sugar and fold in two batches into the previous mix. Fold in the sieved flour with a rubber spatula. Divide the batter in three lined 20 x 20 cm tins. Bake at 200°C in a preheated oven for about 10 minutes and leave to cool.

Praline Lemon: Cook sugar, water and sorbitol to 120°C , preferably in a copper pan Remove from heat and add in the almonds and mix till the almonds are crystallised. Return to medium heat and cook till the almonds are roasted and the sugar is caramelised. Cool on a silicone mat. Blend in a heavy-duty blender till it becomes a smooth paste. Store in a glass jar.

Praline Cream: Soften gelatin in 10 gms cold water and keep aside. Heat cream to 50°C ; add the egg yolks and sugar and heat to 82°C. Sieve and measure 170 gms. Add hydrated gelatin to the measured cream. Mix and then add praline and emulsify with a hand blender. Reserve the remaining cream for any other use.

Blackberry Cream: Heat cream to 50°C ; add the egg yolks and sugar and heat to 82°C. Sieve and add hot blackberry puree and invert sugar. Pour over the chocolate while mixing with a spatula to obtain a smooth, elastic and glossy texture. Give a final mix with a hand blender.

Assembly: Fit one sponge inside a square ring. Spread half the praline cream on top and then place the second sponge. Now spread blackberry cream on top. Place the third layer of sponge and cover with remaining praline cream. Freeze the assembly. Cut into rectangles, sprinkle with Matcha and decorate with almonds and meringues.

MATCHA SURPRISE

Is There Life After Tarts?

CHOCOLATE TEMPTATION

Yield – A 20 cm tart

Chocolate sable
All-purpose flour – 320 gms
Almond powder – 80 gms
Cocoa powder – 30 gms
Baking powder – ½ tsp
Unsalted butter – 200 gms
Fleur de sel – a pinch
Icing sugar – 80 gms
Eggs – 2

Passion fruit ganache
Passion fruit puree – 135 gms
Cream 35% – 70 gms
Honey – 30 gms
Dark chocolate 60-70% – 100 gms
Milk chocolate – 205 gms
Cocoa butter, soft – 10 gms
Unsalted butter, soft – 65 gms

Simple syrup
Caster sugar – 140 gms
Water – 100 gms

Chocolate glaze
Caster sugar – 300 gms
Cream 35% – 300 gms
Simple syrup (recipe below) – 80 gms
Cocoa butter – 10 gms
White chocolate – 120 gms
Dark chocolate, 60-70% – 120 gms
Gelatin powder – 8 gms
Water – 55 gms

Topping
Apricot preserve

Chocolate sable: Mix the butter with the icing sugar; add the dry ingredients previously sifted together, and then the eggs. Leave to rest in the refrigerator for 24 hours, then roll out to 2.5 cm thickness and cut into a 20 cm disc. Bake sable at 160°C in a preheated oven, for about 12 minutes. Make crumble with rest of the sable and bake at 150°C in a preheated oven for 10 minutes.

Passion fruit ganache: Combine the puree, cream and honey and heat to 60°C and pour over the chocolates and cocoa butter; making a core with the hard whisk. Cool to 35°C and add the butter. Pour into 18cm ring molds and freeze.

Simple syrup: Heat sugar and water on low heat till the sugar dissolves. Give one boil and then remove from heat.

Chocolate glaze: Soften gelatin in 40 gms cold water. Caramelise the sugar, deglaze with the cream and the simple syrup. Pour over the chocolate and cocoa butter and emulsify with a hand whisk. Finally add the gelatin, emulsify the mixture with hand blender. Use at 35°C.

Assembly: Unmold the ganache disks. Glaze them and place them on the sable base. Garnish with chocolate decorations and apricot preserve.

DARK PASSION TART

Yield – A 23 cm tart

Chocolate crust
Unsalted butter – 120 gms
Caster sugar – 75 gms
Fleur de sel – a pinch
Vanilla extract – 1 tsp
Egg – 1
Hazelnut flour – 25 gms
All-purpose flour – 120 gms
Cocoa powder – 35 gms

Chocolate cake
Egg whites – 3
Caster sugar – 100 gms
Egg yolks – 3
Vanilla extract – ½ tsp
Cocoa powder, sifted – 30 gms

Topping
Coconut dried, shredded
Strawberries

Passion fruit cream
Cream, 35% – 240 gms
Passion fruit puree – 180 gms
Caster sugar (A) – 75 gms
Egg yolks – 5
Caster sugar (B) – 60 gms
Cornstarch – 35 gms
Milk – 120 gms

Chocolate crust: Sift together the flour and cocoa powder and keep aside. In the bowl of a mixer fitted with paddle attachment, cream butter till light. Add in the sugar, salt and vanilla. Add the egg and then the hazelnut flour. Add sifted flour to the butter mixture. Blend on low speed until just combined. Do not over mix. Chill the dough until firm, approximately 30 minutes. Roll and line a 23 cm tart ring and run a docket to create a few holes. Bake dough at 160°C in a preheated oven, for about 10 minutes, and then cool.

Chocolate cake: In a bowl of a mixer fitted with the whisk attachment, beat the egg whites to soft peaks. Add the sugar and continue whipping to stiff peaks. In a separate bowl, whip the egg yolks to a thick ribbon. When both mixtures have reached the proper consistency, add one-third of the whipped yolks to the egg whites, folding them together using a balloon whisk. Heavy streaks may remain in the batter. Add the remaining egg yolks and gently fold together. Add the vanilla and cocoa powder and continue to fold together until no streaks remain in the batter. Using a piping bag fitted with a large plain tip, pipe the batter onto the parchment-lined sheet pans in a tight spiral pattern in order to form a 23 cm diameter round. Bake at 180°C for approximately 25 minutes until the cake springs back when gently touched. Cool completely and trim to size so that it fits inside the tart.

Passion fruit cream: In a saucepan, bring the cream, passion fruit puree and sugar (A) to a boil. In a separate bowl whisk the egg yolks until smooth. Boil the milk and add the whisked egg yolks. Now pour the egg yolk-milk mixture into the hot cream mix and whisk rapidly for one more boil. Cover the cream with cling film and place in an ice bath to cool the passion fruit cream. Pipe with a star tip on top of the tart. Decorate with toasted coconut flakes and some strawberries.

ORANGE CREPE TART

Yield – A 23 cm tart

Pate sucree
Unsalted butter,
soft – 150 gms
Caster sugar – 75 gms
Egg yolk – 1
Egg – 1
All-purpose flour – 250 gms
Seeds of 1 Vanilla bean
Zest of 1 lemon, grated
Fleur de sel – a pinch

Crepes
Caster sugar – 40 gms
Eggs – 3
Cream, 35% – 60 gms
Milk – 240 gms
All-purpose flour – 110 gms
Vanilla extract – ½ tsp
Fleur de sel – a pinch

Orange caramel sauce
Icing sugar – 200 gms
Fresh orange juice – 180 gms
Grand Marnier – 25 gms
Zest of ½ orange, grated

Orange juice concentrate
Orange juice – 1 litre

Chiboust orange cream
Caster sugar (A) – 20 gms
Cornflour – 25 gms
Egg yolks – 3
Orange juice concentrate –
110 gms (recipe on right)
Cream, 35% – 90 gms
Gelatin powder – 5 gms
Egg whites – 3
Caster sugar (B) – 100 gms

Topping
Orange slices, peeled
Pate sucree crumbled
Pistachios, sliced

Pate sucree: Mix the butter with the sugar, zest and vanilla seeds. Work in the egg and egg yolk and finally the flour and salt. Make a ball, cover with cling film and keep in refrigerator overnight. Roll out to 2-3 mm thickness and line a 20 cm tart ring. Grate the balance dough on a parchment lined tray and bake at 160°C in a preheated oven till golden brown. Cool and use for topping.

Crepes: Stir all the ingredients together except milk until you have obtained a smooth and runny crepe mixture. Then add the milk in small portions to thin this basic mixture Pour the mixture very sparingly into a hot and lightly buttered pan with 20 cm diameter and let it spread to cover the whole pan. Turn the crepe after a few moments and complete cooking on the other side; once done, stack the crepes into a pile.

Orange caramel sauce: Caramelise the sugar until it is golden yellow and then deglaze with the warm orange juice. Then add the grated orange peel and Grand Marnier, and then reduce the sauce until it has reached a slightly syrup-like consistency. Pour the sauce through the strainer into a bowl.

Orange juice concentrate: Pour the orange juice into a plastic, thin-necked jug. Place the jug in the freezer and allow it to freeze completely. Remove the jug and put it upside down over a wide-necked container. Allow the juice to melt and drip into the second container. The water crystals melt slower than the juice, so the initial drips are concentrated orange juice. Discard the plain ice when the drops are no longer orange. Repeating the freeze-and-drip process twice will result in a fine concentrate with minimal water content. Freeze and store the concentrate till ready to use.

Chiboust orange cream: Soften gelatin in 25 gms cold water. Whisk egg whites with the sugar (B) until it forms soft peaks. Mix egg yolks, sugar (A), cornflour, orange juice concentrate and cream with a whisk and then heat, stirring continuously, till it boils Remove from heat and immediately stir in the gelatin and then mix in the beaten egg whites, stirring briefly but vigorously.

Assembly: Place a crepe on the baked tart and brush a little of the Chiboust cream onto the crepe. Add two further layers of crepe and Chiboust, which should reach to the top edge of the tart and keep aside. Now brush the orange caramel sauce on seven of the crepes and then put some blobs of Chiboust orange cream in the centre of the crepes. Fold the edge of these crepes loosely towards the inside and finally drape these with some fancy folds onto the tart.

Decorate the tart with freshly peeled orange slices. Sprinkle a little more of the orange sauce over the crepes. Add a few pistachios and baked pate sucree pieces on top.

ORANGE CREPE TART

RHUBARB TARTLETS

Yield – 8 tartlets

Roasted rhubarb
Rhubarb, fresh – 500 gms
Grenadine syrup – 100 ml

Pâte sablée
All-purpose flour – 250 gms
Fleur de sel – a pinch
Icing sugar – 100 gms
Unsalted butter – 175 gms
Egg yolk – 1
Seeds of ½ Vanilla bean
White chocolate, tempered

Crème diplomat
Gelatin powder – 2 gms
Milk – 125 ml
Ginger, grated – 10 gms
Seeds of ½ Vanilla bean
Egg yolks – 2
Caster sugar – 25 gms
All-purpose flour – 15 gms
Cream 35%, softly whipped – 75 gms

Decoration
Dark chocolate, tempered
Neutral nappage

Roasted rhubarb: Cut the rhubarb into 6 mm batons. Lay the batons out on a baking sheet lined with parchment paper. Brush the rhubarb with the grenadine syrup, then turn over and repeat on the other side. Roast for 5-8 minutes at 170°C in a preheated oven, until soft then leave to cool.

Pate sablee: Place the dry ingredients in a food processor. Add butter and mix until no lumps remain. Add egg yolk and vanilla seeds and mix to form a smooth, homogeneous mass. Shape the dough into a block and wrap in cling film and refrigerate for 2-3 hours. Place the dough on a lightly floured surface and roll out to 3 mm thick and then cut into rectangles of 8 x 5 cm with a serrated edged knife. Prick the base all over, then chill for at least 30 minutes. Blind bake the tarts at 180°C in a preheated oven until golden brown. Leave to cool. Use a pastry brush to cover the base of each tart with the tempered white chocolate, and keep ready.

Crème diplomat: Soften the gelatin in 10 gms cold water and keep aside. Boil milk, infuse with ginger and vanilla for 10 minutes. Strain and keep aside. Whisk egg yolks and sugar till light in colour. Add flour and mix again. Pour the infused milk, and heat and whisk again until it comes to a boil. Reduce the heat and continue to stir and cook for 5-6 minutes. Remove from heat and add gelatin. Cool and then fold in the gently whipped cream. Keep in refrigerator for 30 minutes before use. Spoon it into a piping bag fitted with a 10 mm plain nozzle and pipe on to tart. Refrigerate for 10 minutes. Cut the roasted rhubarb batons into 6.5 cm lengths and then layer them over the top of the tart. Gently warm the nappage in a saucepan and use it to glaze the top of the tarts. Then keep in the refrigerator. Decorate with chocolate and serve.

PEAR TARTLETS

Yield – 8 tartlets

Puff pastry
Unsalted butter, chilled, cubed (A) – 135 gms
All-purpose flour, chilled – 675 gms
Salt – 20 gms
Vinegar, chilled – 20 ml
Water, chilled – 300 ml
Unsalted butter, chilled (B) – 500 gms

Pear filling
Pears, finely diced (A) – 500 gms
Lemon juice – 40 gms
Orange juice – 40 gms
Caster sugar – 50 gms
Brown sugar – 50 gms
Cinnamon, ground – ½ tsp
Pears, finely diced (B) – 300 gms

Classic caramel sauce
Cream, 35% – 180 gms
Caster sugar – 100 gms
Water – 30 ml
Honey – 1 tsp
Unsalted butter, soft – 60 gms
Vanilla extract – ½ tsp

Cordial
Water – 50 gms
Sugar – 50 gms
Citric acid – a pinch

Poppy ice cream
Plain yoghurt – 400 gms
Xantana – 0.5 gms
Icing sugar – 15 gms
Poppy seed extract – 4 drops
Cordial – 50 gms
(recipe on next page)
Poppy seeds – 2 tsp

Puff pastry: Remove the cubed butter (A) from the refrigerator 20 minutes before starting – the butter should be just soft but still very cold so it doesn't melt through the pastry while mixing. Put the butter, flour and salt into the bowl of the food processor and pulse on high for about 30 seconds or until the mixture resembles sand. Combine the vinegar with the chilled water and add to the bowl, pulsing in 3-4 bursts until dough is smooth. Flatten the pastry into a round, flat disc about 2 cm thick. Wrap in cling film and refrigerate for at least 20 minutes or more. Before laminating, or folding the pastry, remove the extra butter (B) from the refrigerator – it should be cold but malleable. Use a rolling pin to gently pound the butter between sheets of baking paper into an 20 cm flat square about 1 cm thick.

Remove the pastry from the refrigerator and roll it out on a lightly floured work surface to make a 20 x 40 cm rectangle. Place the pounded butter at one end of the pastry and fold the other end over to completely enclose the butter.

Turn the pastry 90 degrees and begin to roll it away in the opposite direction in even strokes. When you have a 20 x 90 cm rectangle, fold in both ends to meet in the middle. Fold the pastry in half again to close it, as if one were closing a book. Dust the pastry lightly with flour, cover and refrigerate for 30 minutes. This completes the first fold.

Repeat the folding process three more times to make four folds in total. Each time the pastry is rolled, place it on the bench with the 'book spine' edge running at 90 degrees to the front of the bench on the left-hand side; this will ensure the rotation is at 90 degrees. Refrigerate the pastry for about 30 minutes between each fold to allow the gluten to relax, otherwise it will be hard to roll and the pastry will be more likely to shrink when baked.

Remove the pastry from the refrigerator 30 minutes before finally rolling. Working from the centre of the pastry, gently roll it away in the opposite direction from the bench then turn the pastry 45 degrees and roll out again. Repeat this process until you have a flat rectangular or square disc about 5 mm thick. Refrigerate the pastry for at least 30 minutes. Leave to cool and then use a large round cutter to cut out circles. Spread the rounds on a parchment lined tray, spacing them apart, and bake at 160°C, in a preheated oven, for 20-25 minutes till light brown. Cool on a wire rack.

Pear filling: Bring the orange juice, lemon juice, sugar, and brown sugar to a boil and dissolve thoroughly. Mix the liquid into the finely diced pear (A) and add the ground cinnamon. Pour the mixture out on a tray with silicone mat and bake at 200°C in a preheated oven for 15 to 20 minutes until the pear is lightly caramelised. Mix diced pear (B) with the caramelised pear. Set to cool.

Classic caramel sauce: Bring the cream to a boil in a saucepan over medium heat. Cook the sugar, water, and honey in a heavy-duty saucepan over high heat until the mixture comes to a boil. Brush around the inside of the pan with a damp pastry brush at the point where the sugar syrup meets the sides of the pan. Do this twice during the cooking process to prevent the sugar from crystallizing. Cook the mixture over high heat for about 6-8 minutes, without stirring, until it turns amber colored.

Lower the heat to medium and slowly add the hot cream to the sugar mixture while stirring constantly. The cream will bubble and foam. Continue stirring to make sure there are no lumps. Remove the saucepan from the heat and stir in the butter till it is completely melted. Then stir in the vanilla. Transfer the caramel sauce to a bowl cover tightly with plastic wrap and leave to cool slightly.

Cordial: Boil all ingredients and leave to cool.

Poppy ice cream: Pour yoghurt into a mixing bowl. Stir. Mix xantana with icing sugar and add home made cordial. Pour into the yoghurt and whisk. Add flavoring and poppy seeds. Churn and freeze in any shaped silicone molds.

Assembly: Put the pear filling on top of the baked puff pastry. Layer with a serving of poppy seed ice cream and pour caramel sauce on top. Decorate with chocolate garnish and serve immediately.

SWEDISH OATMEAL TARTLETS

Yield – 36 tartlets

Tart dough
Quick-cooking rolled oats – 80 gms
All-purpose flour – 210 gms
Caster sugar – 100 gms
Unsalted butter – 180 gms
Egg – 1

Chocolate spread
Caster sugar – 300 gms
Liquid glucose – 225 gms
Isomalt – 225 gms
Cream, 35% – 750 gms
Honey – 450 gms
Unsalted butter – 30 gms
Seeds of 2 Vanilla beans
Cocoa paste – 75 gms
Dark chocolate, 60-70% – 120 gms
Milk chocolate – 75 gms

Tart dough: Combine the rolled oats, flour, and sugar in a food processor. Cut the butter into cubes and add to the dry ingredients. Process until the mixture resembles coarse crumbs. Add the egg and mix until the dough holds together; if necessary, add water, 1 teaspoon at a time. On a work surface, roll dough into a strip and cut into 36 equal pieces. Press dough, using thumb dipped in flour, into the greased tartlet pans, making the shell thicker at the edges than at the base. Place tins on a baking sheet. Bake for 12 to 15 minutes until pale golden. Cool and remove from pans by tapping on the bottom of each mold.

Chocolate spread: Combine sugar, glucose and isomalt in a heavy pan. Heat till golden brown. Deglaze with soft butter first and then with previously heated cream, honey and vanilla. Boil once again. Pour over the chocolates and blend using a hand blender. Put the chocolate spread in a piping bag and fill the centre of the tartlets. Put the remaining chocolate spread in jars and close immediately.

COCONUT APPLE TART

Yield – A 26 cm tart

Applesauce
Red apples, peeled – 4
Seeds of 2 Vanilla beans

Sweet pastry dough
Unsalted butter, soft – 125gms
Caster sugar – 120 gms
All-purpose flour – 300 gms
Egg yolks – 5

Topping
Red apples – 3
Apricot jam – 50 gms
Coconut chips – 50 gms
Chia seeds

Applesauce: Cut the apples into small slices, and place them in a pot with vanilla seeds, cook for 30 minutes. Purée the mixture into a smooth applesauce. Chill until ready to use.

Sweet pastry dough: Mix the butter with an electric beater. Add the sugar, the flour and the egg yolks. Knead the ingredients until they are evenly combined. Bring the dough together into a nice, even ball. Wrap in cling film. Chill the dough for two hours until firm.

Lightly flour the work surface, and then roll out the sweet pastry dough to 2 mm thick with a rolling pin. Place the dough in a tart ring. Crimp the edges. Dock the crust by lightly prickling it all over with a fork. Chill the prepared dough in the refrigerator for 1 hour. Pre-bake this tart base at 150°C in a preheated oven for 8 minutes, until it is golden brown. Set aside to cool.

For the apple layer, peel and core the apples, leaving them whole. Use a mandolin to cut the apple into thin rounds. Spread some of the applesauce into the bottom of the pre-baked, cooled tart shell. Arrange the apple slices around the tart in overlapping concentric circles.

Bake the tart at 180°C in a preheated oven for 5 minutes. Set aside to cool.

Topping: Heat apricot jam in 2 tbsp of water and sieve. Brush the top of the tart with this. Sprinkle coconut chips and chia seeds on top to decorate. Serve at room temperature.

CHOCOLATE HEART ATTACK

Yield – 4 tartlets

Pate sablee
Unsalted butter,
soft – 200 gms
Icing sugar – 100 gms
Fleur de sel – a pinch
Seeds of 1 Vanilla bean
Zest of ½ orange, finely grated
Eggs – 2
All-purpose flour – 200 gms
Cocoa powder – 50 gms
Cocoa butter, for coating

Chocolate and passion fruit mousse
Passion Fruit puree – 100 gms
Cream, 35% – 60 gms
Liquid glucose – 50 gms
Milk chocolate,
chopped – 220 gms
Gelatin powder – 4 gms
Cream, 35%, softly
whipped – 200 gms

Orange caramel sauce
Icing sugar – 200 gms
Orange juice, freshly
squeezed – 180 gms
Cointreau – 25 gms
Zest of ½ orange, grated

Passion fruit ice cream
Milk – 250 gms
Caster sugar – 50 gms
Invert sugar – 8 gms
Atomized glucose – 30 gms
Cream, 35% – 80 gms
Milk powder – 20 gms
Ice cream stabilizer – 2.5 gms
Egg yolks – 2
Passion fruit puree – 215 gms

Apricot jam
Fresh apricots,
pitted – 350 gms
Caster sugar – 250 gms
Pectin HM – 3 gms
Citric acid – ⅛ tsp
Orange juice – 100 ml
Juice of ½ lemon
Seeds of ½ Vanilla Bean

Cocoa caviar
Water – 250 gms
Sugar – 50 gms
Agar agar – 2 gms
Cocoa powder – 30 gms
Sunflower oil – 1 litre

Pate sablée: Put the butter, sugar and salt in a bowl of a stand mixer with paddle attachment and cream together for about 5 minutes, or until it becomes a pale cream colour. Add the vanilla seeds and orange zest into the creamed butter mixture. Add the orange zest and mix. Gradually add the eggs, whisking all the time until fully incorporated. Gently mix in the flour and cocoa powder, taking care not to overwork the dough. Bring the dough together and form a ball. Wrap in cling film, flatten into a disc and chill for at least two hours.

When ready to prepare, roll out the dough to a thickness of about 2 mm on a lightly floured surface. Neatly line the tart pans with the pastry and trim off any excess from around the edges with a small, sharp knife. Prick the base with a fork and chill in the refrigerator for 20 minutes.

Line the tarts with baking parchment, fill with baking beans and bake blind on a baking sheet at 170°C, in a preheated oven, for about 20 minutes or until pale golden. Remove from the oven and discard the parchment and beans. Return the tarts to the oven and continue to cook for a further 5 minutes, or until crisp. Remove from the oven and set aside to cool. Brush with a little melted cocoa butter on the inside to seal the tart from humidity of the mousse.

Chocolate and passion fruit mousse: Soften gelatin in 20 gms cold water. Heat the puree with cream and liquid glucose. Add gelatin and mix. Pour over milk chocolate. Leave it undisturbed for a few minutes. Now mix with spatula and cool to 35°C. Fold in whipped cream. Put in piping bag and pipe in a spiral on the baked tart. Sift cocoa powder on top.

Orange caramel sauce: Heat orange juice, mix orange zest and keep aside. Caramelise sugar in a heavy-duty pan. Deglaze with orange juice and Cointreau. Reduce to syrup like consistency. Pour the same through a strainer into a bowl.

Passion fruit ice cream: Mix half the sugar with stabilizer. Heat the milk and cream. At 25°C, add the milk powder, half the sugar and glucose. At 35°C, add egg yolks and invert sugar. At 45°C, add the mix of sugar and stabilizer. Cook this to 85°C and then cool rapidly to 4°C. Add the puree and mix using a hand blender. Refrigerate overnight. Churn in ice cream machine and store in freezer for use.

Apricot jam: Mix sugar with pectin and citric acid and add all the ingredients into a large pan set over a medium heat and cook to 112°C. Remove from the heat and set aside for 2-3 minutes before pouring into sterilized glass jars. Secure the lid on tightly, turn the jar upside down and leave to cool completely.

Cocoa caviar: Combine all the ingredients except the sunflower oil. Bring to a boil while continuously stirring to prevent the cocoa from sticking to the bottom of the saucepan. Leave to cool to 70°C. Separately, half fill a rectangular container, (approximately 7 cm in height), with oil. Fill a syringe with the cocoa base and drip the content into the oil. Allow the caviar drops to gel and settle at the bottom of the container before pouring new drops. Take out the caviar and rinse in warm water.

Assemble all the components individually on a platter in a decorative manner.

CHOCOLATE HEART ATTACK

WILD BERRY TARTLETS

Yield – 12 tartlets

Cocoa pate sablee
Unsalted butter – 185 gms
All-purpose flour – 250 gms
Seeds of 1 Vanilla bean
Hazelnut powder,
toasted – 100 gms
Cocoa powder – 25 gms
Salt – ¼ tsp
Egg whites – 4
Icing sugar – 135 gms
Cocoa butter, melted

Sponge cake with hazelnuts
Eggs – 5
Caster sugar – 115 gms
Invert sugar – 12 gms
Zest of 1 lemon
Fleur de sel – a pinch
All-purpose flour – 115 gms
Hazelnut flour – 75 gms
Unsalted butter,
melted – 30 gms
Frangelico Liqueur – 50 gms

Wild berry jam
Wild berries – 450 gms
Orange juice – 50 gms
Lemon juice – 2 tbsp
Caster sugar – 200 gms
Yellow pectin – 5 gms

Lemon curd
Gelatin powder – 2 gms
Lemon juice – 150 gms
Eggs – 2
Honey – 180 gms
Unsalted butter,
melted – 75 gms

Mascarpone bavarian
Cream 35%, softly
whipped – 320 gms
Gelatin powder – 12 gms
Caster sugar – 140 gms
Egg whites – 6
White chocolate,
melted – 115 gms
Mascarpone cheese – 340 gms

Cocoa pate sablee: Rub the butter in with the flour, vanilla and salt. Add the hazelnut powder with the cocoa, followed by the egg whites and the icing sugar. Knead until the dough is smooth and firm. Make a ball and cover with a cling film. Leave to rest in the refrigerator overnight. Remove from fridge and roll cut to 2.5 mm thickness. Line the tartlet pans.

Prick the base of each tartlet with a fork, refrigerate for 20 minutes. Cover the tartlets with parchment and fill with baking beans. Bake at 170°C, in a preheated oven, for 10 minutes or until pale golden. Remove from oven, lift out the baking beans with parchment and bake for another 2-3 minutes. Cool and then brush with melted cocoa butter.

Sponge cake with hazelnuts: Heat eggs, sugar, lemon zest and salt to 50°C. Place in a stand mixer and whip using a whisk until the mixture is voluminous and stable. Fold in all-purpose flour and hazelnut flour delicately. Remove 1/10 of the mixture and to this add the melted butter, then carefully add to the rest of the mixture. Pour on a 1 cm high baking sheet lined with parchment and bake at 170°C in a preheated oven for about 15-20 minutes. Cool on a wire rack. Sprinkle with Frangelico liqueur and cut into rounds to fit inside the tarts.

Wild berry jam: Combine the berries, orange juice, and lemon juice; stir to coat berries. In a small bowl, whisk together the sugar and pectin. Cover the berry mixture with the pectin and sugar. Use a rubber spatula to press down on the fruit; this will break down the berries and incorporate the sugar-pectin. Over medium heat, cook the mixture for 3 to 5 minutes, stirring continuously. When the berries begin to release their juices, turn up the heat so that the mixture comes to a boil. Allow it to boil for 4 to 6 minutes, stirring occasionally and scraping the bottom so that the jam doesn't burn.

Pour the hot berry jam into a glass bowl and let it cool to room temperature. Cover the jam with cling film and let it sit for 1 hour or more until the jam has a glossy, thick, jelly consistency. Pour over the sponge cake to reach the top of the tartlets.

Lemon curd: Soften the gelatin in 10 gms cold water. Put the lemon juice in a pan over a medium heat and warm through. In a mixing bowl, whisk the eggs and add the honey and then pour into the pan with the lemon juice. Bring to the boil, stirring all the time. Cook for one minute then remove from the heat and then add gelatin. Again, bring to the boil, then cool it down to about 40°C. Add the butter and stir until completely melted. Mix with a hand blender. Pipe with a plain tip into a small doughnut shape in a silicone mold and freeze.

Mascarpone bavarian: Soften gelatin in 60 gms cold water and keep aside. Beat egg whites and sugar over a bain-marie, whisking constantly till the temperature reaches 60°C. Remove from heat and continue whisking till stiff peaks are formed. Melt the gelatin and add to the chocolate, then quickly stir the chocolate mixture into one-third of the meringue mixture to temper it. Still working quickly, add this to the remaining meringue. Mix the cream into the mascarpone cheese and fold into the meringue.

Immediately divide the prepared Bavarian cream among the round silicone molds. Insert a frozen lemon curd doughnut and press lightly. Cover with some more Bavarian cream. Spread the tops even and freeze. Unmold the above assembly, and place over the jam on the tart. Decorate as desired with meringues.

CHOCOLATE CHERRY TARTLETS

Yield – 12 tartlets

Hazelnut sable
All-purpose flour – 150 gms
Hazelnut powder – 50 gms
Ground cinnamon – ½ tsp
Fleur de sel – a pinch
Unsalted butter,
cubed – 100 gms
Icing sugar – 25 gms
Egg – 1

Hazelnut ganache
Cream, 35% – 75 gms
Dark chocolate, 60-70% –
175 gms
Honey – 20 gms
Hazelnut paste – 50 gms

Cherry jam
Cherry purée – 150 gms
Cherries, pitted – 150 gms
Caster sugar – 120 gms
NH pectin – 20 gms
Lemon juice – 10 ml

Chocolate caramel tuile
Liquid glucose – 90 gms
Caster sugar – 180 gms
Dark chocolate, 60-70%,
chopped – 120 gms

Custard
Milk – 250 gms
Cream, 35% – 60 gms
Seeds of ½ Vanilla bean
Zest of ½ lemon
Caster sugar – 60 gms
Egg yolks – 7
Corn starch – 15 gms
Rice flour – 10 gms
Fleur de sel – a pinch

Topping
Chocolate tuile
Gold powder
Cherries, fresh

Hazelnut sable: Tip the flour and hazelnut powder into the bowl of a food processor, add the cinnamon, salt and butter. Pulse to rub the butter into the flour until it's pale and sand-like in texture. Add the icing sugar and mix again to combine. Add the egg and pulse until the mixture starts to come together. Tip the dough out onto the work surface and using hands, bring dough together into a neat ball. Flatten into a disc, cover in cling wrap and chill in the fridge for at least one hour until firm.

Roll the dough out on a lightly floured work surface to a thickness of 2 mm. Using a cookie cutter stamp out 12 discs from the dough. Gently press the discs into the tartlets trying not to stretch the dough but making sure that it is evenly lined. Chill in the fridge for 20 minutes.

Line the tart cases with a square of baking parchment and fill with baking beans. Bake tarts at 170°C in a preheated oven for 10 minutes until pale golden and just starting to crisp. Remove the tarts from the oven and carefully lift out the baking beans and parchment and return the pans to the oven for one more minute to dry out the tart bases. Remove from the oven and leave to cool before removing sable from the pan.

Hazelnut ganache: Place all the ganache ingredients into a heatproof bowl and set over a pan of barely simmering water. Stir gently to combine ingredients to a silky, smooth mixture, remove from the heat and leave to cool for 15 minutes. Transfer to a piping bag and set aside.

Cherry jam: Put the cherry purée, cherries and 75 gms of sugar in a heavy-based saucepan and bring to the boil. Mix the remaining sugar with the pectin in a small bowl. Whisk the pectin mixture into the boiling liquid. Continue to cook over a low heat, stirring continuously until the mixture reaches 104°C. Add the lemon juice and continue to cook for a further 2-3 minutes. Pour the jam into a sterilized jar and leave to cool before closing the lid.

Chocolate caramel tuile: Bring the glucose to a boil in a saucepan. Add the sugar and stir to combine and then let it boil to 168°C without stirring. Remove from heat and stir in the chocolate. Immediately roll the mixture between two silicone mats to a thickness of about 2 mm. Once cooled, use a rolling pin to grind to a fine powder. Sift the caramel powder on a silicone mat about 1 mm thick. Bake at 200°C for about 5 minutes in a preheated oven until the caramel starts to liquidify. Upon removal from the oven, shape the chocolate caramel brittle into uneven curves, by rolling around a tube shape, made of parchment paper.

Custard: Mix starch, rice flour, sugar, and salt and egg yolks. Separately, heat the milk, cream, vanilla seeds, lemon zest and half the sugar. When the milk starts to boil, pour slowly over the starch mix. Heat again and cook until boiling. Pour onto a tray lined with baking paper, cover and cool in the refrigerator.

Assembly: To build the tarts, divide and spread the cherry compote between pastry cases and level. Pipe ganache over the cherry compote in an even, smooth layer. Finish with a thin layer of custard. Decorate with fresh cherries. Sprinkle icing sugar on top of chocolate tuile and some gold powder on cherries.

CHOCOLATE CHERRY TARTLETS

CHOCOLATE ALMOND TARTLETS

Yield – 6 tartlets

Tarts
All-purpose flour – 125 gms
Fleur de sel – a pinch
Unsalted butter – 60 gms
Icing sugar – 15 gms
Lemon juice – 1 tbsp

Filling
Egg – 1
Caster Sugar – 90 gms
Cocoa powder – 12 gms
Almond flour – 90 gms
Cream – 50 gms
Apricot jam – 80 gms
Almonds – 16

Feel free to use any jam if apricot jam is not available.

Tarts: Process flour, salt, butter and icing sugar in a food processor until the mixture resembles fine breadcrumbs. Add juice and process until the mixture forms a ball. Roll out dough between two sheets of baking paper to 3 mm thickness. Cut into rounds with fluted cutter. Place in the tart tins and chill for 20 minutes.

Filling: Beat egg and sugar until thick and pale. Sift cocoa on top. Stir in the almond flour and cream. Place a dot of jam in each tart. Spoon the filling in and place an almond in the centre. Bake tarts at 180°C in a preheated oven, for 15 minutes until the top of the filling is puffed and set. Leave to cool in the tins for 5 minutes then turn out onto wire racks.

PRALINE & COCOA NIB TARTLETS

Yield – 12 tartlets

Pate sucree
All-purpose flour – 190 gms
Icing sugar – 70 gms
Almond flour – 25 gms
Unsalted butter, soft – 115 gms
Seeds of ½ Vanilla bean
Egg – 1

Hazelnut praline
Caster sugar – 50 gms
Sorbitol powder – 5 gms
Water – 20 gms
Hazelnuts – 90 gms

Crunchy praline
Hazelnut praline – 150 gms (recipe on right)
Milk chocolate, melted – 15 gms
Cocoa butter, melted – 15 gms
Paillete feuilletine – 60 gms

Chocolate dentelle
Hazelnuts, toasted, chopped – 40 gms
Caster sugar – 75 gms
Unsalted butter – 60 gms
Liquid glucose – 25 gms
Milk – 20 gms
Cocoa nibs – 40 gms
Cocoa powder – 7 gms

Chocolate ganache
Dark chocolate, 60-70%, melted – 200 gms
Cream, 35% – 170 gms
Honey – 15 gms
Liquid glucose – 10 gms
Unsalted butter, soft – 15 gms

Pate sucree: Mix flour, almond flour and half the icing sugar together. Place the butter in the bowl of a stand mixer fitted with the paddle attachment and cream on medium-low speed. Sift in the remaining icing sugar and vanilla seeds and pulse to begin incorporating the sugar, then increase the speed to medium-low and mix for about 1 minute, until the mixture is fluffy. Add the flour mix and then the egg. Combine lightly. Make a ball. Cover with cling film. Refrigerate until firm for two hours or preferably overnight.

Roll the dough to 2 mm thickness. Cut into rounds and line the small tart molds. Line the dough with parchment paper and baking beans. Bake at 180°C for six minutes and turn down the oven to 160°C. Remove the beans and parchment paper, return to oven and bake for 4-5 minutes longer until it is baked through and light golden brown. Leave to cool on a wire rack.

Hazelnut praline: Roast the hazelnuts at 150°C for 10-12 minutes. Heat water, sorbitol and sugar to 185°C. Remove from heat, mix hazelnuts and spread on a silicone mat to cool. Blend in a powerful, sturdy blender making sure the praline does not heat up.

Crunchy praline: Mix all the ingredients in a bowl. Place a large piece of parchment paper on the work surface. Spoon the mixture into the centre and top with a second piece of parchment. Roll the praline to under 3 mm thick. Slide the praline in the paper onto a sheet pan. Freeze until solid, at least four hours. Cut into circles to fit inside the tarts.

Chocolate dentelle: Heat sugar, butter, glucose and milk in a saucepan and stir over medium-high heat until the mixture reaches 110°C. Remove from heat and stir in the hazelnuts, cocoa nibs and cocoa powder. Pour the mixture onto a piece of parchment paper and top with a second sheet. Roll out as thin as possible. Transfer it, still in the parchment paper, to a sheet pan. Remove the top piece of parchment and bake at 180°C in a preheated oven. After a few minutes, the mixture will begin to bubble. When the bubbles size becomes smaller, remove from the oven and set on a cooling rack. Cut the dentelle into pieces and use later to garnish the tarts.

Chocolate ganache: Heat the cream, honey and glucose in a saucepan and bring to a simmer over medium heat, stirring to combine the ingredients. Remove from the heat, pour one-third of the mixture over the chocolate, and stir from the centre, incorporating the chocolate from around the edges of the bowl. Repeat with the remaining cream. The ganache should be shiny and smooth. Stir in the butter and mix. Pour the ganache into the tart shell, on top of the crunchy praline and let it set at room temperature for at least four hours. Garnish with pieces of dentelle.

PRALINE & COCOA NIB TARTLETS

SUMMER BREEZE TART

Yield – A 26 cm tart

Coconut shortbread
All-purpose flour – 260 gms
Icing sugar – 105 gms
Almond powder – 15 gms
Coconut powder – 15 gms
Unsalted butter – 150 gms
Fleur de sel – a pinch
Egg – 1
Zest of 2 lemons

Almond coconut cream
Unsalted butter – 60 gms
Caster sugar – 60 gms
Almond powder – 30 gms
Coconut powder – 30 gms
Egg – 1
Dark rum – 1 tbsp

Pineapple cardamom jam
Cubed pineapple
pieces – 250 gms
Caster sugar – 200 gms
Seeds of 1 Vanilla bean
Green cardamom,
crushed – 1 tsp
Juice of 3 lemons
Rapid-set pectin – 1.5 gms

Coconut and lime tuile
Caster sugar – 75 gms
NH pectin – 3 gms
Unsalted butter – 60 gms
Liquid glucose – 25 gms
Coconut, dried,
shredded – 80 gms

For topping
Kiwis
Physalis
Strawberries
Pomegranate seeds
Oranges

Coconut shortbread: Mix all the dry ingredients and lemon zest. Blend in the cubed butter, till crumbly. Add egg and mix till homogenized. Make a ball. Cover with cling film and refrigerate for one hour. Roll to 2.5 mm thickness circle and line the tart ring. Reserve in refrigerator for one hour. Bake at 160°C in a preheated oven and then let it cool completely.

Almond coconut cream: Mix the soft butter and sugar. Add the almond and coconut powder and egg. Mix till homogenized. Add rum and mix again. Cover with cling film and refrigerate for about one hour before using.

Pineapple cardamom jam: Mix pineapple with 150 gms sugar and crush lightly by hand. Mix in vanilla, green cardamom, lemon juice and zest. Give one boil. Refrigerate overnight. Mix the remaining sugar with the pectin. Once again, crush the pineapple lightly with hand blender. Add the pectin to the mix. Boil rapidly and cook to 105°C. Cool before using.

Coconut and lime tuile: Bring sugar, pectin, butter and glucose to a boil. Add grated coconut. Roll between two sheets of greaseproof paper to a thickness of 1.5 mm. Bake at 150°C in a preheated oven. Cut out discs of 7 cm with a round biscuit cutter.

Assembly: Spread the coconut almond cream on the baked tart ring. Bake at 160°C for about 20 minutes till the top is a golden brown. Let it cool. Spread the pineapple cardamom jam and arrange the fruits on top. Decorate with coconut and lime tuile. Sprinkle icing sugar on top.

Seasonal fruits can replace fruits mentioned in the recipe for a change.

SUMMER BREEZE TART

RASPBERRY CLOUD TARTLETS

Yield – 6 tartlets

Pate sucree
Unsalted butter – 150 gms
Caster sugar – 75 gms
Egg – 1
Egg yolk – 1
All-purpose flour – 250 gms
Zest of 1 lemon, grated
Fleur de sel – a pinch

Raspberry chocolate cremeux
Egg yolks – 3
Egg – 1
Caster sugar – 40 gms
Raspberry puree – 170 gms
Gelatin powder – 4 gms
Milk chocolate – 110 gms

Raspberry jelly
Raspberry puree – 330 gms
Icing sugar – 20 gms
Lemon juice – 15 gms
Gelatin powder – 6 gms

Almond sponge crust
Marzipan – 175 gms
Eggs – 4
Egg yolk – 1
Caster sugar – 55 gms
All-purpose flour – 50 gms
Baking powder – ½ tsp
Unsalted butter,
melted – 70 gms
Fleur de sel – a pinch
Vanilla extract – 1 tsp
Zest of 1 lemon, grated

Meringue mixture
Egg whites – 8
Caster sugar – 400 gms

Pate sucree: Mix the butter with sugar and lemon zest. Work in the egg and egg yolk and finally the flour and salt. Make a ball and cover with cling film. Refrigerate overnight. Roll to 2 mm thickness and cut into rounds to fit inside the tart rings. Bake blind at 160°C till the pate is golden brown.

Raspberry chocolate cremeux: Soften gelatin in 20 gms cold water. Heat puree, sugar, egg yolks and egg in a bowl and set over a saucepan of simmering water. It is important that the base of the bowl does not touch the water. Whisk continuously and heat to 80°C. Remove from heat, add gelatin and mix. Strain this mix over the chocolate and then blend to a smooth and homogeneous mixture. Fill the mixture into baked tarts. Refrigerate.

Raspberry jelly: Soften gelatin in 30 gms cold water. Heat a small part of the raspberry puree with icing sugar and lemon juice. Add the gelatin. Mix in the remaining puree. Pour this on top of the cremeux in the tarts and the remaining in small decorative silicone molds, for decoration.

Almond sponge crust: Sieve flour with baking powder and salt. Add the eggs and the egg yolk to marzipan and carefully work to a smooth consistency. Then add the sugar, zest and vanilla and temper the mixture to about 35°C and beat very well in the bowl of a stand mixer with whisk attachment, until frothy. Mix in first the flour and then the hot butter (45°C). Spread on a sheet pan of 1 cm height lined with parchment. Bake the crust at 175°C for about 20-25 minutes till golden. Cool on a wire rack and cut into rounds to fit on top of the tarts.

Meringue mixture: Heat up egg whites with the sugar to approximately 50°C and then beat stiff until cold Heating up the mixture of the egg white and sugar is necessary in order to obtain a sticky mixture and high viscosity. This produces a stable and firm meringue mixture.

Topping: Cover the surface of the well-cooled raspberry tart with the meringue mixture and level the edge as well as the surface smooth for flaming. Add a circle of meringue mixture using round piping tip no. 8. Dust lightly with icing sugar and then using a blowtorch, flame until the desired colour is achieved. Finally decorate the tarts in the centre with some raspberry jelly and raspberry flakes.

PASSION FRUIT TARTLETS

Yield – 20 tartlets

Sweet shortcrust pastry
Unsalted butter, chilled, cubed – 200 gms
Vinegar, chilled – 10 ml
Caster sugar – 50 gms
Water, cold – 80 ml
All-purpose flour – 330 gms
Fleur de sel – a pinch

Passion fruit bavarois
Milk – 300 ml
Gelatin powder – 8 gms
Egg yolks – 6
Caster sugar – 175 gms
Passion fruit juice – 250 ml
Cream, 35% – 350 gms

Italian meringue
Caster sugar – 200 gms
Water – 100 ml
Egg whites – 4

Topping
Passion fruit seeds

Sweet shortcrust pastry: Put the vinegar and sugar in a bowl and add the water, stirring well. Set aside for 10 minutes, and then stir again to completely dissolve the sugar. Put the flour and salt in the bowl of the food processor and add the butter, pulsing in 1-second bursts for about three or four times to partly combine the ingredients.

Turn out onto a clean work surface and gather together. Sprinkle the sugar mixture and mix gently. Shape into a round, flat disc about 2 cm thick. Cover with cling wrap and refrigerate for at least two hours or preferably overnight. Remove the pastry from the refrigerator 20 minutes before rolling it out. Roll to 2-3 mm thickness and again keep in refrigerator for 2 hours. Now cut and line the tart rings with the dough. It is important not to stretch the dough when lining the tins. Again freeze the lined tart rings for 10-20 minutes. Bake the tart rings at 200°C in a preheated oven for 15-20 minutes, or until golden brown. Remove from the oven and leave to cool.

Passion fruit bavarois: Soften the gelatin in 40 gms cold water. Just about boil the milk in a saucepan over high heat. Whisk the egg yolks, sugar and passion fruit together in a bowl. Sit the bowl over a saucepan of simmering water; making sure the base of the bowl does not touch the water. Add the hot milk and continue whisking for about 5 minutes, or until the mixture is quite thick. Whisk in gelatin into the passion fruit mixture. Strain through a fine sieve and refrigerate for 30 minutes to one hour or until it is just starting to set.

Whip the cream to soft peaks, and then fold through the passion fruit mixture, taking care not to over whip the cream or it will not fold through easily. Pour the bavarois carefully into the pastry shells, filling them to the brim. Place in the refrigerator for 2-3 hours or until set.

Italian meringue: Put the sugar and water in a small heavy-based saucepan over high heat. Bring to the boil, stirring along the way. Just as it is starting to boil stop stirring as this will cause sugar crystals to form. Brush the sides of the saucepan with a wet pastry brush every couple of minutes or when you see crystals starting to form. Allow the mixture to reach 118°C on the thermometer then remove from the heat immediately.

Put the egg whites in a clean bowl of a stand mixer fitted with a whisk attachment. Mix on high speed for about two minutes, or until foamy, then add the extra sugar and whisk until soft peaks form. With the mixer still running on high, slowly pour the sugar syrup. Once added, turn the mixer to low speed and continue mixing for a further 10-15 minutes, or until the meringue is cool.

Assembly: Completely cover the top of the tart with the bavarois. Use a piping (icing) bag; pipe the meringue onto the top of the bavarois. Brown the meringue with a blowtorch. Decorate with some passion fruit seeds.

CAKES

You Bake Me Happy

CHOCOLATE TRUFFLE CAKE

Yield – A 20 cm round cake

Brownie
Dark chocolate, 60-70% – 50 gms
Unsalted butter – 25 gms
Brown sugar – 50 gms
Vanilla extract – 3 tsp
Egg yolk – 1
All-purpose flour – 50 gms
Brandy – 50 ml

Dark chocolate cream
Dark chocolate, 60-70% – 400 gms
Cream 35% – 400 gms
Brandy – 25 ml
Vanilla extract – 2 tsp

White chocolate cream
White chocolate – 600 gms
Cream – 35% 400 gm
Brandy – 25 ml
Vanilla extract – 2 tsp

Glazing
Dark chocolate – 100 gms
Hot black coffee – 50 ml
Cocoa powder

Brownie: In a saucepan, gently melt the chocolate and butter, then stir in first the sugar and vanilla, then the egg yolk and flour. Mix well, then spoon into the base of the greased mold and bake at 180°C in a preheated oven for 15 minutes until set. Remove from the oven and if the brownie has puffed up, prick with a fork and press flat with a tea towel. Before it cools sprinkle with brandy.

Dark Chocolate cream: Melt the chocolate in a saucepan with half the cream. Add brandy and vanilla. Separately beat the remaining cream until lightly thickened but still pourable. Add the chocolate to the beaten cream and stir until just smooth. Spoon this on to the brownie base and leave to chill.

White Chocolate cream: Repeat the above process with the white chocolate to make the second layer. When ready pour over the dark chocolate layer.

Glazing: Melt the chocolate, stir in the hot coffee until smooth, and pour over the assembled cake and leave to set.

To release the cake from the mold, run a hot knife around the outside, or use a kitchen blowtorch on the mold, then dust with sieved cocoa powder. Garnish with chocolate decorations as desired.

NUTTY BANANA CAKE

Yield – A 16 x 8 cm loaf

Caramelised hazelnuts
Hazelnuts, chopped – 200 gms
Caster sugar – 80 gms
Water – 30 gms
Unsalted butter – 5 gms

Lime syrup
Caster sugar – 85 gms
Water – 175 gms
Lime zest – 4 gms

Banana cake
Unsalted butter, soft – 85 gms
Icing sugar – 130 gms
Fleur de sel – a pinch
Eggs – 2
All-purpose flour – 155 gms
Baking powder – 6 gms
Potato starch – 10 gms
Bananas, puréed – 180 gms
Caramelised hazelnuts, chopped – 40 gms
Zest of 1 lime
Milk chocolate – 50 gms
Milk – 70 gms
Lime syrup – 60 gms
(recipe on right)

Chocolate cremeux
Cream 35% – 325 gms
Invert sugar – 10 gms
Gelatin powder – 5 gms
Dark chocolate, 60-70% – 120 gms
Milk chocolate – 115 gms

Chocolate hazelnut glaze
Milk chocolate, melted – 350 gms
Grape seed oil – 100 gms
Caramelised hazelnuts, chopped – 100 gms
(recipe on right)

Caramelised hazelnuts: Roast the chopped hazelnuts at 155°C in a preheated oven for five minutes. Mix sugar and water and cook to 118°C in a large pan. Add hot nuts and caramelise slowly. First it will become sandy and then it will start to caramelise. Stir to avoid burning. Cook at medium temperature to prevent the heat penetrating the nuts. Finally, add butter and cool it down on silicone mat. The caramelised hazelnuts will be used for the cake as well as the glaze.

Lime Syrup: Boil all the ingredients together and strain and keep aside.

Banana cake: Sieve flour, baking powder and potato starch together. For ganache pour hot milk over milk chocolate. Leave for two minutes and mix with hand blender. Cream the butter with icing sugar and salt in a bowl of stand mixer. Add eggs, one by one. Add sieved flour and lime zest. Add bananas and then ganache gradually. Add 42 gms of caramelised hazelnuts. Mix well. Pipe into the greased and parchment-lined mold.

Bake at 150°C in a preheated oven for 30 minutes and remove from tin after two minutes. Let it cool. Take 60 gms of warm lime syrup. Apply with brush only on sides of the cake. Freeze after cooling.

Chocolate cremeux: Soften gelatin in 25 gms of cold water. Heat cream and invert sugar to 82°C. Add the gelatin and strain. Pour out over chocolates and make an emulsion with hand blender. Cool to 30°C, before using. Pour on the centre of the frozen cake or alternatively spread on top of the frozen cake. Re-freeze the cake.

Chocolate hazelnut glaze: Mix milk chocolate, oil and caramelised hazelnuts. Use at 28°C on frozen cakes. With a ladle, pour the glaze on cakes. Keep in fridge for 10 minutes. Apply glaze again a second time. Decorate with chocolate and remaining hazelnuts.

BUTTERSCOTCH CAKE

Yield – A 30 x 10 cm loaf

Walnuts – 160 gms
All-purpose flour – 270 gms
Baking powder – 1 tsp
Fleur de sel – ¼ tsp
Unsalted butter, soft – 250 gms
Brown sugar – 180 gms
Eggs – 4
Cream 35% – 50 gms
Vanilla extract – 2 tsp

Toast the walnuts at 160°C in a preheated oven for eight minutes. Cool on a rack then coarsely chop the walnuts. Sift the flour and baking powder. Add the salt and toss to blend well. Beat the butter in the bowl of a stand mixer using the paddle attachment until fluffy. Add the brown sugar and beat together well. Stop occasionally and scrape down the sides and bottom of the bowl with a rubber spatula

Add the eggs, one at a time, blending well after each addition. Add the cream and vanilla to the mixture, blending well. Add the flour mixture in three stages, blending well after each addition. Then stir in the walnuts, mixing thoroughly.

Pour the cake batter into the prepared pan, smoothing the top with a rubber spatula. Bake at 160°C in a preheated oven for approximately one hour, or until the cake is light golden and a skewer inserted in the centre comes out clean. Remove the pan from the oven and cool on a rack. Serve at room temperature.

ORANGE HAZELNUT CAKE

Yield – A 23 x 10 cm loaf

Cake
Caster sugar – 225 gms
Oranges – 5
Unsalted butter – 100 gms
Ginger, fresh, peeled and finely grated – 10 gms
Cream, 35% – 75 gms
Eggs – 3
All-purpose flour – 325 gms
Baking powder – 3 tsp

Topping
Hazelnuts, chopped
Cinnamon powder
Candied ginger
Orange, sliced

Cake: Finely grate the zest from the oranges and set aside. Put the sugar in a saucepan, squeeze 150 ml juice from the oranges and pour in with the sugar. Bring to a boil, remove from the heat and add the butter. Leave for five to ten minutes to cool and for the butter to melt, and then stir in the zest, ginger and cream. Beat in the eggs, and then stir in the flour and baking powder until smooth.

Spoon cake mix into the greased loaf tin, sprinkle with chopped hazelnuts and cinnamon. Bake for 50 minutes or until a skewer pulls out cuite clean.

Decorate with candied ginger and orange slices.

CHOCOLATE FONDANT

Yield – A 20 cm round cake

Chocolate sable
Unsalted butter, soft – 200 gms
Icing sugar – 70 gms
Fleur de sel – a pinch
All-purpose flour – 160 gms
Cocoa powder – 25 gms

Strawberry coulis
Strawberry puree (A) – 130 gms
Liquid glucose – 30 gms
Caster sugar – 30 gms
Pectin NH – 4 gms
Strawberry puree (B) – 125 gms

Chocolate ganache
Dark chocolate 60-70% – 100 gms
Unsalted butter – 25 gms
Egg yolks – 2
Egg – 1
Cream 35% – 125 gms

Liquid chocolate
Dark chocolate 60-70%, melted – 70 gms
Unsalted butter, clarified – 80 gms
Egg whites – 5
Caster sugar – 110 gms
Fleur de sel – a pinch
Egg yolks – 4
Corn starch – 30 gms
Almond powder – 30 gms
Cocoa powder – 15 gms

Topping
Coco nibs, caramelised
Icing Sugar
Cocoa powder

Chocolate dough: Mix butter, sugar and salt. Add the sifted flour and cocoa powder. Make a soft dough. Pipe with a piping bag in a spiral on the bottom of the cake ring, placed on a silicone mat. Bake at 145°C in a preheated oven for 25 minutes.

Strawberry coulis: Combine the sugar and the pectin and keep aside. Heat the strawberry puree (A) and then glucose. Now add the pectin mix. Cook to 103°C. Add the strawberry puree (B) and boil. Cool and then refrigerate. Pipe on top of baked tart and then chill in refrigerator.

Chocolate ganache: Heat the chocolate and butter to 65°C. Whisk in the egg yolks and egg. Add the cold cream in three batches. Pipe on top of coulis.

The beauty of this fondant lies in its multiple textures.

Liquid Chocolate: Melt the chocolate and the butter to 65°C. Whip the egg whites, sugar and salt in a separate bowl. Mix the egg yolks with the chocolate. Add the sifted corn starch, almond flour and cocoa powder. Fold in the beaten egg white and sugar. Pipe on the ganache. Bake at 180°C in a preheated oven for 15 minutes.

Finish by decorating with caramelised cocoa nibs, icing sugar and cocoa powder.

MARBLE CAKE

Yield – A 30 x 12 cm loaf

Marble cake
All-purpose flour – 180 gms
Baking powder – ½ tsp
Eggs – 4
Caster sugar – 200 gms
Fleur de sel – a pinch
Cream 35% – 90 gms
Unsalted butter, melted – 60 gms
Cocoa powder – 15 gms

Citrus syrup
Juice of 2 oranges
Juice of 1 lime
Caster sugar – 30 gms

Marble cake: Butter and flour the loaf pan and keep ready. Sift the flour and baking powder into a bowl. Put the eggs, sugar and salt in another large bowl and beat using a stand mixer for a good 8 to 10 minutes until it is really light and foamy. Fold in the cream, then add the sifted flour and baking powder and fold gently together. Finally fold in the melted butter. Transfer one-third of the batter to another bowl. Sift the cocoa powder into the remaining batter and mix gently until all the cocoa is combined.

Put half of the cocoa mixture into the bottom of the prepared cake pan then add the plain batter and finish with the remaining cocoa batter. Hold knife or skewer along one side of the pan and using a folding action, gently swirl the knife / skewer from left to right down the length of the pan. This will give you a great marbled effect.

Bake the cake at 160°C in a preheated oven for 25 to 30 minutes until a skewer inserted into the middle comes out clean.

Citrus syrup: Put all the syrup ingredients in a small saucepan over low heat and let the sugar dissolve completely. Turn the heat up to medium and cook until there is about two tablespoons syrup which is thick enough to coat the back of a spoon. Remove the pan from the heat and leave to one side.

Remove the cake from the oven and put the pan on a wire rack to cool for five minutes. Turn the cake out of the pan and drizzle the citrus syrup over the top. Leave to cool before slicing and serving.

FINNISH TEA CAKE

Yield – A 20 cm round cake

Coffeebread
Active dry yeast – 7 gms
Water – 250 ml
Egg – 1
Caster sugar – 50 gms
Salt – ½ tsp
Milk – 125 ml
Unsalted butter, melted – 60 gm
All-purpose flour – 250 gms

Apple and plum jam
Apples, peeled and cored – 225 gms
Plums, pitted – 450 gms
Water – 45 ml
Caster sugar – 650 gms

Topping and decoration
Almonds flour – 50 gms
Caster sugar – 75 gms
Unsalted butter, soft – 100 gms
All-purpose flour – 40 gms
Almonds, slivered – 50 gms
Icing sugar – 80 gms

Coffeebread: In a large bowl, dissolve the yeast in the warm water. Let it stand for five minutes. Add the egg, sugar, salt, and lukewarm milk. Stir in the butter and half the flour. Beat till smooth. Add the remaining flour and beat again until smooth. Cover and let it rise in a warm place until doubled, for about one hour.

Apple and plum jam: Chop the peeled and cored apples; halve the plums. Put the fruit into the preserving pan with water. Simmer gently until the fruit breaks into a soft puree, then add the sugar and stir over a low heat until this has dissolved. Raise the heat and boil rapidly to 102°C or 62°Brix on a refractometer. If there are large pieces of fruit in the jam, cool slightly then stir briskly to distribute the fruit. Spoon into jars and seal.

Topping: Process the almond powder, sugar, butter and flour in a mixer until the mixture is a smooth paste. Roll the risen dough into a circle and put on a greased baking sheet. Spread with the topping mixture. Sprinkle with slivered almonds. Bake at 190°C in a preheated oven for 20 minutes until crust is golden. Remove from oven and drizzle with icing sugar on the sides. Serve with apple and plum jam.

NOTHING BUT CHOCO CAKE

Yield – A 18 x 10 cm loaf

Cake
Cocoa powder – 25 gms
Water – 150 ml
Dark chocolate 60-70%, melted – 60 gms
Baking soda – ½ tsp
Unsalted butter, soft – 125 gms
Muscovado sugar – 150 gms
Condensed milk – 125 ml
Eggs – 2
Vegetable glycerine – 2 tsp
All-purpose flour – 200 gms
Baking powder – 2 tsp

Hot caramel fudge sauce
Caster sugar – 100 gms
Cream 35% – 250 gms
Vanilla extract – 1 tsp
Dark chocolate 60-70% – 240 gms

Decoration
Chocolate shavings
Icing sugar

Cake: Line the bottom and sides of the loaf pan with parchment paper. Sift flour and baking powder and keep aside. Warm the water and mix with cocoa to make a smooth paste. Immediately stir in the chocolate and baking soda and leave it to melt. In the bowl of a stand mixer beat the butter, sugar and condensed milk with the paddle attachment until very smooth, then beat in the eggs and glycerine. Stir in half the sifted flour and baking powder into the egg mixture, followed by adding the chocolate mixture, then beat in the remaining flour and mix until smooth.

Scrape the mixture evenly into the pan and bake at 180°C in a preheated oven for 40 to 50 minutes or until a skewer in the centre comes out clean. Leave to cool in the pan and peel off the parchment paper once the cake has cooled down.

Hot caramel fudge sauce: Cook sugar in a saucepan over medium-high heat until golden brown. In a separate pot, warm cream with vanilla over medium heat. Carefully pour cream into caramelised sugar and bring to a boil. Stir until mixture is smooth and glossy. Pour this through a sieve over the dark chocolate (in a bowl) and let melt. Mix with spatula until smooth. Pour the sauce over the cake. Garnish with chocolate shavings and dust with icing sugar, if desired.

LEMON LOAF CAKE

Yield – A 25 x 8 cm loaf

Eggs – 5
Caster sugar – 240 gms
Cream 35% – 140 gms
Fleur de sel – ¼ tsp
All-purpose flour – 245 gms
Baking powder – 1 tsp
Unsalted butter, soft – 110 gms
Grapeseed oil – 20 gms
Seeds of 2 Vanilla beans
Zest of 2 lemons

Sift flour with baking powder and keep aside. In a bowl of a stand mixer, whisk the eggs and the sugar. Add the cream, the salt and lemon zest. Whisk well. Fold in the sifted flour.

Melt 70 gms butter slightly in the microwave, add the neutral oil and the vanilla seeds. Fold in to the egg mixture while making sure the batter is smooth and homogeneous.

Pour in the greased and lined loaf tin. Soften the 40 gms butter and put in piping bag with plain tip. Pipe in the centre of cake mix. Bake at 140°C in a preheated oven for about an hour till a skewer inserted in the centre comes out clean. Leave to cool in the tin for 10 minutes. Then remove on a wire rack and cool completely.

COCONUT CHOCOLATE BOURBON CAKE

Yield – A 33 x 10 cm loaf

Cake
Dark chocolate 60-70%, melted – 150 gms
Unsalted butter, soft – 150 gms
Cream cheese, soft – 100 gms
Sunflower oil – 30 gms
Caster sugar – 250 gms
Eggs – 3
Seeds of 1 Vanilla bean
Coconut, dried, shredded – 75 gms
Milk – 75 gms
All-purpose flour – 275 gms
Baking powder – 3 tsp

Chocolate bourbon glaze
Caster sugar – 100 gms
Cocoa powder – 10 gms
Milk – 50 gms
Unsalted butter – 20 gms
Dark chocolate 60-70%
Bourbon – 15 ml

Decoration
Coconut chips
Chocolate shavings
Icing sugar

Cake: Line the base and sides of the loaf tin with parchment paper. Sift flour and baking powder and set aside. Beat the butter, cream cheese, oil and sugar for about three minutes until very light and fluffy. Whisk in the eggs one at a time until smooth then beat in the vanilla seeds. Beat in the coconut and milk then fold in the sifted flour.

Divide the mixture into two bowls, and stir the melted chocolate into one of the portions. Scoop alternate spoonfuls of the vanilla and chocolate mixtures into the loaf tin then gently swirl the batter with a butter knife. Bake at 160°C in a preheated oven for about an hour or until a skewer inserted in the centre comes out clean. Leave to cool in the mold.

Chocolate bourbon glaze: Put the sugar, cocoa, milk and butter in a saucepan, stir well and bring to boil. Cook to 108°C. Remove from the heat, and wait for the bubbling to stop and then stir in the chocolate. Mix until smooth. Add the bourbon and stir through. Leave to slightly cool, stirring often until it's thick enough to sit on the top of the cake as well as drizzle down the sides. Leave until the glaze is cool.

Decorate with chocolate shavings and coconut chips. Sprinkle icing sugar on top.

ORANGE ROSEMARY CAKE

Yield – Two 18 cm round cakes

Cake
Oranges – 2
Baking powder – 1 tsp
Eggs – 6
Caster sugar – 220 gms
Fine semolina – 150 gms
Fresh rosemary, finely chopped – 1½ tsp
Almond powder – 150 gms

Rosemary syrup
Oranges – 2
Caster sugar – 110 gms
Water – 125 ml
Lemon juice – 1½ tbsp
Grand Marnier – 30 ml
Fresh rosemary, few sprigs

Cake: Place unpeeled oranges in a medium saucepan over high heat, cover with cold water; bring to the boil for about an hour or until oranges are tender. Drain and cool. Trim and discard ends from oranges. Halve oranges; discard seeds. Process orange, including rind, with baking powder until mixture is pulpy. Transfer to a large bowl. Whip eggs and sugar until thick and creamy. Stir egg mixture into orange mixture. Fold in semolina, almond powder and rosemary. Spread mixture into greased pans.

Bake at 180°C in a preheated oven for one hour or until a skewer inserted into the centre comes out clean. Stand cake in pan for 45 minutes before turning top-side up onto a cake plate.

Rosemary syrup: Peel the rinds of oranges into wide strips with a vegetable peeler, and then cut them into thin strips. Place sugar, water and lemon juice in a small saucepan over low heat; stir, without boiling, until sugar dissolves. Add thin strips of rind, bring to the boil; for five minutes or until syrup thickens. Remove from heat; stir in liqueur and rosemary sprigs.

Spoon the hot syrup over the freshly baked cakes. Ideally, the cakes should be served warm or at room temperature.

PLUM & LEMON CAKE

Yield – A 23 cm round cake

Vanilla-poached plums
Plums – 1200 gms
Caster sugar – 110 gms
Lemon rind, finely grated – 2 tsp
Vanilla extract – ½ tsp

Cake
Almond flour – 110 gms
Coconut, dried and shredded – 100 gms
Polenta – 125 gms
Baking powder – 1 tsp
Unsalted butter, soft – 225 gms
Caster sugar – 220 gms
Lemon rind, finely grated – 1 tbsp
Eggs – 4
Limoncello – 60 ml

Polenta is Italian maize that gives the cake its pleasant crunch.

Vanilla-poached plums: Halve the plums, remove the stones and cut each half into these wedges. Place plums and other ingredients in a medium-based saucepan over low heat; cover and cook for 10 minutes, shaking pan occasionally, till plums start to soften and release juice. Remove lid; cook a further seven minutes, shaking pan occasionally, or until syrup reduces and thickens slightly, then cool.

Cake: Mix almond flour, coconut, polenta and baking powder in a medium bowl. Beat butter, sugar and rind in the bowl of a stand mixer with paddle attachment until pale and fluffy. Beat in eggs, one at a time, until well combined. Fold in combined dry ingredients until mixture just starts to come together. Add Limoncello; mix until just combined. Spread half the cake mixture into greased and lined pan.

Drain 450 gms of the vanilla-poached plums; arrange plums evenly on cake mixture. Dollop remaining cake mixture over plums then gently spread to cover plums. Bake at 170°C in a preheated oven for 1¼ hours or until a skewer inserted into the centre comes out clean. Stand cake in pan 15 minutes before transferring to a wire rack to cool. Place cake on plate; dust with icing sugar. Top the cake with remaining plums and syrup.

COCONUT & MARMALADE CAKE

Yield – A 23 x 10 cm loaf

Cake
Sunflower oil – 90 ml
Orange juice, fresh – 120 ml
Orange marmalade – 80 gms
Eggs – 2
Zest of 2 oranges, grated
Caster sugar – 35 gms
Coconut, dried,
shredded – 35 gms
All-purpose flour – 45 gms
Semolina – 90 gms
Almond powder – 15 gms
Baking powder – 1 tsp

Soaking syrup
Caster sugar – 100 gms
Water – 70 ml
Orange blossom water – 1 tsp

Cake: Whisk together the oil, orange juice, marmalade, eggs, and orange zest until the marmalade dissolves. In a separate bowl, mix together all the dry ingredients and add to the marmalade mixture. Mix until well combined. Pour the batter on a greased and lined loaf pan. Bake at 180°C in a preheated oven for 45 to 60 minutes, until a skewer inserted into the cake comes out clean and the top turns an orangey-brown.

Near the end of the baking time, place the syrup ingredients in a small saucepan and bring to a boil, then remove from the heat. As soon as the cake is out of the oven, using a pastry brush start coating the cake with the hot syrup, allowing the syrup to soak in for a minute or two before starting the next coat. Make sure all the syrup is absorbed into the cake. Once the cake has cooled down a little, remove from pan and leave to cool completely.

ANISEED AND ORANGE CAKE

Yield – A 35 x 7 cm loaf

Cake
Semi-candied orange – 100 gms
Whole eggs – 4
Caster sugar – 180 gms
All-purpose flour – 200 gms
Unsalted butter,
melted – 200 gms
Aniseed – 5 gms

Candied orange
Orange, sliced – 1
Orange juice – 100 gms
Caster sugar – 100 gms
Seeds of 1 Vanilla bean

Orange frosting
Orange marmalade – 100 gm

Cake: Beat the eggs with the sugar in the bowl of a stand mixer with whisk attachment for 10 minutes. Fold in the flour. Add in the melted butter and mix the aniseeds and the chopped semi-candied orange. Pour into the greased and lined loaf tin and bake at 160°C in a preheated oven for 30-40 minutes. Leave to cool.

Candied orange: Bring the orange juice with the sugar and vanilla seeds to a boil. Pour on the orange slices. Leave to marinate overnight.

Orange frosting: Heat the marmalade with 1 tbsp water.

Assembly: Spread the orange frosting with a brush on the top and sides of the cake. Arrange the candied orange slices on top. Sprinkle with a few silver coated aniseeds.

APRICOTS CARDAMOM SAVARIN

Yield – A 23 cm ring cake

Savarin
Instant dry yeast – 7 gms
Milk, lukewarm – 60 gms
Caster sugar – 30 gms
Eggs, beaten lightly – 4
All-purpose flour – 260 gms
Fleur de sel – 1 tsp
Unsalted butter (A), soft – 100 gms
Unsalted butter (B), melted – 20 gms

Apricots in dessert wine syrup
Orange – 1
Dessert wine – 750 ml
Water – 500 ml
Caster sugar – 550 gms
Cardamom pods, bruised – 10
Apricots, dried – 185 gms

Savarin: Combine yeast, milk and 1 teaspoon of the sugar in a small bowl; cover, stand in a warm place 10 minutes or until frothy. Stir in egg. Combine flour, salt, cardamom and remaining sugar in a bowl of a stand mixer fitted with a dough hock. Add yeast mixture; mix on medium speed for three minutes or until dough is smooth and elastic. Scrape down the side of bowl with a spatula; cover, stand in a warm place for one hour or until dough has doubled in size.

Return the bowl with the risen dough to the stand mixer fitted with the dough hook. Add chopped butter to dough, a few pieces at a time, beating on medium speed, for two minutes or until smooth and elastic. Spoon dough mixture into a disposable piping bag; pipe mixture into buttered pan. Cover loosely; stand in a warm place for 45 minutes or until mixture is almost doubled in size. Bake at 220°C in a preheated oven for 25 minutes or until golden and a skewer inserted into the centre comes out clean. Stand savarin in pan for five minutes.

Apricots in dessert wine syrup: Using a vegetable peeler or a zester, peel rind from orange avoiding white pith; cut into thin strips. Place rind, wine, water, sugar and cardamom in a medium saucepan; bring to the boil, stirring to dissolve sugar. Simmer for two minutes. Add apricots to syrup. Remove from heat; cover and keep aside. Strain apricots from syrup, and keep aside apricots, rind and cardamom. Pour 750 ml of the syrup slowly over the savarin in the pan until syrup is absorbed. Stand savarin in pan for 10 minutes to soak in the syrup, before turning out onto a cake plate.

Meanwhile, simmer remaining syrup in a small saucepan over medium heat for eight minutes or until thickened. Return reserved apricots, rind and cardamom to thickened syrup. Cool. Drizzle the concoction over the savarin, which can be served warm or at room temperature.

UPSIDE DOWN BANANA CAKE

Yield – A 20 cm square cake

Cake

Unsalted butter, soft – 100 gms
Maple syrup – 160 gms
Bananas, ripe – 4
Dark brown sugar – 200 gms
Eggs – 4
Vanilla extract – 2 tsp
All-purpose flour – 200 gms
Baking powder – ½ tsp
Walnuts, chopped – 100 gms
Baking soda – 1 tsp
Cinnamon powder – 1 tsp
Greek yoghurt – 200 gms

Caramel sauce

Walnuts – 100 gms
Salted butter, cubed – 100 gms
Cream 35% – 100 gms
Maple syrup – 120 gms

Cake: Grease and line a square tin with parchment. Pour in 60 gms of maple syrup, swirling to coat the bottom. Peel and halve the three ripe bananas lengthways and lay, cut-side down, in the tin. Sift flour and baking powder and keep aside. Beat together the butter, sugar, eggs, vanilla and one banana in the bowl of a stand mixer with whisk attachment. Tip the flour and walnuts into a food processor and pulse until finely ground together. Stir into the beaten butter mixture with the baking soda and cinnamon, and then stir in the yoghurt. Carefully spoon into the pan without dislodging the bananas. Bake at 150°C in a preheated oven for about one hour until a skewer inserted in the centre comes out with a few moist crumbs.

Caramel sauce: Toast the walnuts for 1-2 minutes in a pan, add the remaining ingredients and cook until the butter has melted. Then let it bubble for five minutes until thick.

Once the cake is cooked, poke it all over with the skewer – inserting it about halfway into the cake each time. Pour the remaining half of the maple syrup over the cake and allow it soak in for a few minutes, then turn the cake out of the tin, upside-down, onto a serving plate. Serve with the sauce.

CHOCOLATE & TAMARIND CAKE

Yield – A 28 x 6 cm cake

Streusel
Caster sugar – 40 gms
Unsalted butter,
soft – 40 gms
Almond flour – 15 gms
All-purpose flour – 15 gms
Dark chocolate, 60-70%,
melted – as required

Tamarind cremeux
Orange juice – 65 ml
Tamarind puree – 50 ml
Egg – 1
Egg yolks – 2
Unsalted butter – 55 gms
Gelatin powder – 3 gms
White chocolate, melted – 10 gms

Caramelized bananas
Caster sugar – 60 gms
Bananas, sliced – 2
Dark rum – 60 ml
White wine – 60 ml

Milk chocolate mousse
Milk – 100 ml
Caster sugar – 10 gms
Egg yolk – 1
Gelatin powder – 3 gms
Milk chocolate – 240 gms
Cream, 35%, softly
whipped – 220 gms

Milk chocolate glaze
Cream, 35% – 100 gms
Caster sugar – 25 gms
Liquid glucose – 30 gms
Water – 20 ml
Milk chocolate – 300 gms
Cocoa butter – 50 gms
Dark rum – 45 ml

Streusel: Mix all the ingredients, except chocolate, in a blender. Make a ball. Cover with cling film and leave in refrigerator overnight. Remove from refrigerator and grate roughly on a parchment lined baking tray. Bake streusel at 160°C in a preheated oven, for about 15 minutes. Cool and coat with melted chocolate.

Tamarind cremeux: Soften gelatin in 15 gms cold water. Heat orange juice, tamarind puree, egg and egg yolks and whisk over bain-marie till well heated and is light and fluffy. Remove from heat and add the butter, chocolate and gelatin. Mix with hand blender. Pour in an insert mold and freeze.

Caramelised bananas: Heat sugar in a sauce pan and caramelise. Add bananas in a single layer. Add rum and wine and cool till the liquid dries up. Put the bananas over the frozen tamarind cremeux and freeze again.

Milk chocolate mousse: Soften gelatin in 15 gms cold water. Whisk egg yolk and sugar, pour milk over it and heat. Cook this, stirring continuously, till it reaches 85°C. Add gelatin and mix well. Pour through a strainer over the chocolate. Let it sit undisturbed for two minutes. Now, start mixing with a spatula from the centre.

When blended, cool to 35°C and then fold in whipped cream. Pour some mousse in the mold. Put the frozen insert of cremeux and banana, with the cremeux side up. Put some more mousse on top. Cover with chocolate-coated streusel to level off with the top of the mold and freeze. Pour rest of the mousse into truffle shaped silicone molds and freeze.

Milk chocolate glaze: Heat cream, sugar, glucose and water. Add chocolate and cocoa butter and cook for two minutes. Remove from heat and add rum. Mix with a hand blender and refrigerate. Use at 50°C.

Assembly: Remove the cakes from the molds. Keep it upside down and glaze. Glaze the mousse truffle balls too and keep on top of cake. Decorate on top with chocolate-coated streusel and chocolate decorations.

TROPICAL CAKE

Yield – A 23 cm round cake

Dacquoise
Egg whites – 8
Caster sugar – 125 gms
Icing sugar – 110 gms
Coconut, dried, shredded – 110 gms
All-purpose flour – 60 gms
Unsalted butter, melted – 25 gms

Streusel
Almond powder – 75 gms
Brown sugar – 75 gms
Unsalted butter – 75 gms
All-purpose flour – 75 gms

Herb sponge
Eggs – 3
Caster sugar – 250 gms
All-purpose flour – 250 gms
Baking powder – 8 gms
Milk – 250 ml
Olive oil – 175 gms
Mint, fresh – 10 gms
Basil, fresh – 10 gms

Italian meringue
Sugar – 185 gms
Water – 100 ml
Liquid glucose – 50 gms
Egg whites – 125 gms

Coconut mousse
Coconut puree – 250 gms
Italian meringue – 100 gms, (recipe on right)
Gelatin powder – 4 gms
Cream 35%, softly whipped – 250 gms

Mango and passion fruit mousse
Mango purée – 375 gms
Passion fruit purée – 190 gms
Gelatin powder – 15 gms
Caster sugar – 75 gms
Italian meringue – 260 gms, (recipe on right)
Cream 35%, softly whipped – 375 gms

White chocolate spray
White chocolate, melted – 200 gms
Cocoa butter, melted – 150 gms

Dacquoise: Sieve flour and icing sugar and mix in coconut and keep aside. Whip the caster sugar and egg whites until stiff in the bowl of a stand mixer with whisk attachment on medium speed. Fold in the flour mix and finally add the butter. Bake at 180°C in a preheated oven in 20 cm rings for 8 to 10 minutes.

Streusel: Gently combine all the ingredients until a homogeneous mixture is obtained. Reserve in refrigerator overnight. Grate the cough on a parchment lined sheet. Pour the streusel without pressing too much on a 20 cm ring and bake at 150°C in a preheated oven for 15 minutes.

Herb sponge: Puree the mint and basil together with olive oil. Beat the eggs and sugar to a ribbon stage. Add the milk and the oil and herb mixture and finally the flour together with the baking powder. Keep it in refrigerator overnight. Slightly beat so as to extract all the gas. Add the batter over the baked streusel and bake at 180°C in a preheated oven for eight minutes.

Italian meringue: Cook the water, sugar and glucose to 121°C. Pour over the whipped egg whites and whip to a completely fluffy texture. Use lukewarm.

Coconut mousse: Soften gelatin in 20 gms cold water. Heat the puree and add gelatin. Cool to 28°C and fold in the meringue. Lastly, fold in the whipped cream gently and use immediately. Pour over the baked dacquoise and freeze.

Mango and passion fruit mousse: Soften gelatin in 75 gms cold water. Combine both purées and heat small amount together with the sugar so as to dissolve the melted gelatin. Add the remaining purée. Once the mixture is at 28°C, add some of the cream and make an emulsion. Gently fold in the already-made meringue, making sure it holds the texture, and finish with the remaining cream. Use immediately.

Assembly: Arrange a 23 cm wide ring and start by pouring in a first layer of mango and passion fruit mousse. Place the coconut insert then add another layer of mousse. Finish with the streusel and herb sponge. Freeze the assembly.

White chocolate spray: Remove the assembly from the ring and place it upside-down. Mix white chocolate and cocoa butter and spray on the frozen cakes.

TROPICAL CAKE

ROSE LOAF CAKE

Yield – A 23 x 10 cm loaf

Rose syrup – 40 gms
Whole milk – 30 ml
Almond flour – 200 gms
Icing sugar – 160 gms
Eggs – 4
Caster sugar – 35 gms
Unsalted butter, soft – 185 gms
Rose extract – ¼ tsp
All-purpose flour – 80 gms
Strawberries, quartered – 175 gms

Mix the rose syrup and milk and separately mix almond flour and icing sugar. Separate three eggs into whites and yolks. In a bowl of a stand mixer fitted with the whisk attachment, beat the egg whites just until they start to hold their shape, then gradually add the caster sugar, beating until the whites hold firm, glossy peaks.

Put the butter and almond-flour mixture in the mixer bowl, using the paddle attachment beat at medium-high speed, until very smooth. Working at medium speed, add the three egg yolks one at a time, beating for about one minute after each addition, then beat in the one whole egg. Add the rose-flavoured milk, as well as the rose extract, and beat for one more minute.

Stir a little of the whisked egg whites to the batter to lighten it. Then fold the remaining whites and the all-purpose flour into the batter; folding in the flour in about three additions and the whites in two.

Scrape one third of the batter into the parchment lined loaf pan and evenly spread it. Make three rows of strawberries down the length of the pan – don't let the berries touch the sides of the pan – then cover the berries with half of the remaining batter and bake at 150°C in a preheated oven for about an hour, or until a skewer inserted into the centre comes out clean. The top of the cake should be a lovely brown and springy to the touch and the cake should have started to pull away from the sides of the pan. Transfer the cake to a cooling rack and let it rest for about three minutes, then unmold it, invert it, and let it cool to room temperature on the rack.

Decorate with frosted rose petals or as desired.

MANGO HAZELNUT & CHOCOLATE CAKE

Yield – A 23 cm round cake

Hazelnut cake
Egg yolks – 3
Egg – 1
Caster sugar – 55 gms
Egg whites – 3
Caster sugar – 35 gms
Unsalted butter, melted – 35 gms
Hazelnuts, toasted and powdered – 100 gms
All-purpose flour – 15 gms

Crumble
Unsalted butter – 55 gms
Light brown sugar – 65 gms
All-purpose flour – 65 gms
Fleur de sel – 2 gms

Reconstituted crumble
Milk chocolate, melted – 15 gms
Unsalted butter, melted – 10 gms
Hazelnut praline – 15 gms
Crumble – 125 gms
(recipe on next page)

Salted caramel
Caster sugar – 100 gms
Cornflour – 10 gms
Milk – 35 gms
Cream 35% – 100 gms
Liquid glucose – 10 gms
Fleur de sel – a pinch
Seeds of 1 Vanilla bean
Gelatin powder – 2 gms
Salted butter – 35 gms

Mango jelly
Mango puree – 250 gms
Lemon juice – 25 gms
Caster sugar – 10 gms
Gelatin powder – 4 gms

Vanilla cremeux
Cream 35% (A) – 450 gms
Xantana – 0.5 gms
Caster sugar – 50 gms
Gelatin powder – 5 gms
Cream 35%, whipped (B) – 150 gms

Chocolate mousse
Milk – 160 gms
Cream 35% (A) – 25 gms
Seeds of 1 Vanilla bean
Gelatin powder – 5 gms
Milk chocolate – 260 gms
Cream 35%, whipped (B) – 350 gms

Chocolate glaze
Water – 150 gms
Sugar – 125 gms
Liquid glucose – 150 gms
Milk powder – 10 gms
Condensed milk – 125 gms
Gelatin powder – 10 gms
Milk chocolate – 150 gms

Hazelnut cake: Whisk the egg yolks, egg and sugar till light and fluffy. Separately, make a meringue with egg whites and sugar. Add melted butter to the egg yolk mix. Mix the meringue and egg-yolk mix and then fold in the flour and hazelnuts. Pour the mixture on a baking sheet of 1 cm height. Bake at 200°C in a preheated oven for about 10-12 minutes. Once it is cold, cut a round of 20 cm diameter.

Crumble: Place all the ingredients in a food processor and mix. Spread on a parchment lined tray and bake at 160°C in a preheated oven for 10-12 minutes.

Reconstituted crumble: Mix the melted chocolate, butter and praline. Add salted crumble (as above) and mix. Roll out thin discs 20 cm in diameter and freeze.

Salted caramel: Mix corn flour with milk. Soften gelatin powder in 10 gms cold water. Heat cream, glucose, vanilla and salt. Remove from heat and mix corn flour and milk mixture. Caramelise sugar in a heavy-duty pan. Deglaze with cream mix. Boil and remove from heat. Add gelatin and cool to 45°C. Add butter and mix with hand blender. Spread on top of hazelnut cake and freeze.

Mango jelly: Soften gelatin in 20 gms cold water. Heat puree, lemon juice and sugar. Add gelatin and mix. Pour into 20 cm round silicone molds and freeze.

Vanilla cremeux: Soften gelatin in 25 gms cold water. Mix cream (A) and xantana with a hand blender and then heat in a saucepan. Add sugar and gelatin. Mix with rest of the cream. Cool to 20°C. and then fold in the whipped cream (B). Pour over the frozen mango jelly and freeze.

Chocolate mousse: Soften gelatin in 25 gms cold water. Boil the milk and cream (A) with vanilla. Add gelatin. Pour over chocolate and mix with hand blender. Cool to 30°C. Then fold in whipped cream (B) and use immediately.

Chocolate Glaze: Soften gelatin in 50 gms cold water. Boil water, sugar, glucose and milk powder. Remove from heat and mix condensed milk and gelatin. Pour over chocolate and mix with hand blender. Cover with cling film and refrigerate overnight. Use at 28°C over frozen cake.

Assembly: Place a 23 cm ring on to a tray and build the cake upside down. Firstly add a layer of the chocolate mousse in the bottom of the mold. Then add in the disc of frozen mango jelly and vanilla cremeux. Again add a layer of mousse. Now put the sponge with salted caramel, sponge side up. Again spread some more mousse on top; and lastly add the frozen reconstituted sable.

Freeze the assembly. After unmolding turn the cake upside down and glaze and decorate as desired.

NUTELLA & RICOTTA CALZONE

Yield – 4 calzones

Calzone
Strong flour – 500 gms
Dry yeast – 2 gms
Cold water – 300 ml
Salt – 15 gms

Filling
Nutella – 290 gms
Ricotta cheese – 500 gms

Topping
Nutella
Icing sugar

Calzone: Mix all the ingredients in a bowl of stand mixer with a dough hook and knead for 10-15 minutes. Cover and leave to rest for 10 minutes before kneading again for 10 seconds. Divide the dough into four pieces and leave to rest overnight in a sealed container, covered in cling film. Remember to leave space for each of your dough balls as these will double in size because of the yeast. After proving, the dough balls are ready to use straight away. Roll into 26 cm round.

Filling: Warm the Nutella over a pan of hot water to make it easier to work. Divide into the four batches and spread on top of dough bases and dot with dollops of fresh ricotta. Fold the dough in half and press along the edges to make a good seal before baking for 4-5 minutes in a preheated oven at 230°C. Once out of the oven, drizzle a little more Nutella and dust with icing sugar.

FRUIT & FENNEL CAKE

Yield – 12 mini loaves

Fennel seeds, roasted – 1 tsp
Unsalted butter, soft – 125 gms
Seeds of ½ Vanilla bean
Zest of 1 lemon
Zest of 1 orange
Caster sugar – 225 gms
Fleur de sel – a pinch
Eggs – 3
Cream cheese – 120 gms
All-purpose flour – 160 gms
Baking powder – ½ tsp
Plums or apples, sliced – 2

Topping
Neutral glaze
Pistachios, slivered
Fennel seeds, silver coated

Any soft stone fruit can be used instead of apple or plum to add a twist.

Sift the flour and baking powder. Beat the butter, vanilla seeds, zest, fennel seeds, sugar and salt together until just combined. (Don't overbeat). Add the eggs one at a time, mixing each egg in well, so that the batter is completely smooth before the next goes in. Add the cream cheese, sifted flour in one go and mix at full speed for a few seconds to make sure everything is well combined.

Divide the batter between the greased and parchment lined mini loaf pans. Top each cake with four or five plum or apple slices spread out like a small fan and sprinkle with additional sugar.

Bake loaves at 170°C in a preheated oven for 20-25 minutes till it is a lovely golden colour. Brush with neutral glaze and sprinkle pistachios or silver coated fennel seeds on top.

PEAR & HAZELNUT CAKE

Yield – A 20 cm round cake

Brownie
Unsalted butter,
soft – 130 gms
Dark chocolate 60-70% –
80 gms
All-purpose flour – 50 gms
Hazelnuts, toasted and
chopped – 40 gms
Eggs – 3
Caster sugar – 85 gms
Brown sugar – 85 gms

Caramel spread
Caster sugar – 80 gms
Cream 35% – 200 gms
Liquid glucose – 10 gms
Fleur de sel – a pinch
Dark chocolate 60-70% –
40 gms

Caramelised pears
Pears, peeled and cored – 4
Caster sugar – 175 gms
Water – 210 ml

Pear cream
Caramelised pear pieces –
160 gms (recipe on right)
Milk – 70 gms
Egg yolks – 4
Caster sugar – 40 gms
Cream 35% – 140 gms
Gelatin powder – 5 gms

Pear jelly
Caramelised pear – 90 gms
(recipe on right)
Sugar syrup – 30 gms
Agar agar – 0.5 gms
Gelatin powder – 5 gms

Crumble
Hazelnuts, roasted &
chopped – 60 gms
Hazelnuts, ground – 40 gms
Rice flour – 60 gms
Muscovado sugar – 30 gms
Brown sugar – 10 gms
Unsalted butter,
cubed – 40 gms

Chocolate mousse
Cream 35% (A) – 50 gms
Milk – 40 gms
Egg yolks – 2
Honey – 20 gms
Chocolate 60–70%,
chopped – 125 gms
Gelatin powder – 5 gms
Cream 35%, whipped (B) –
180 gms

Brownie: Line a 30 cm x 40 cm baking tray with parchment paper. Melt the butter and chocolate together to 50°C. Add the flour, then the chopped hazelnuts, ensuring all are well incorporated.

Place the eggs and both sugars in the bowl of a stand mixer and whisk on high speed until thick and foamy, about eight minutes. Add the chocolate mixture, while continuing to whisk on high speed. Pour the mixture into the prepared tray and spread it evenly. Bake at 160°C in a preheated oven for 20 minutes or till a light crust has formed on top. The cake should still be moist when tested with a skewer. Remove from the oven and allow the cake to cool in the tray before turning it out onto a wire rack. Once the cake is cool, cut out a disk of 16 cm for the base.

Caramel spread: Caramelise sugar in a heavy pan till it is golden in colour. Place the cream, glucose and salt in a medium saucepan over medium heat. Bring the mixture to just below boiling then remove from the heat. Pour the cream mixture into the hot caramelised sugar to deglaze. Once all of the cream and caramel are well mixed, turn the heat to low and reduce the volume of mixture by half, stirring occasionally. Place the chocolate in a large mixing bowl and strain the hot caramel mixture on top. Stir gently with a hand whisk to form a homogenous mass. Cover with cling film and leave the mixture to cool.

Caramelised pears: Mix the sugar and the water together and pour over the quartered pears that have been placed on a tray. Place a sheet of baking paper over the pears, then lay a sheet of foil on top of the paper and crimp the edges to seal the tray. Bake at 160°C in a preheated oven for 45 minutes. Remove the tray from the oven and leave to cool naturally with the foil still on.

Once cool, remove the foil and drain the cooking liquid into a medium saucepan. Place the saucepan over medium heat and bring the liquid to a boil till the liquid is reduced to a thick syrup. Once it starts to turn golden, place the cooked pear quarters into the pan. Cook the pears for one minute, and turn them over using a fork. Remove the pan from the heat and allow the pears to cool in the syrup. Cut the cooled pears into bite-sized chunks and keep in an airtight container in the fridge until needed.

Pear cream: Soften gelatin in 25 gms cold water. Puree the caramelised pears in the blender to get a smooth paste. Place the puree, milk, egg yolks and sugar in a saucepan over medium heat. Heat the mixture to 85°C , stirring constantly. Remove the pan from the heat and add the cream to the mixture. Stir well, and then transfer this mixture to a single loaf pan.

Place the pan in the oven and bake at 200°C in a preheated oven for 16-20 minutes. The custard will overcook and start to separate and also begin to colour on top. When some dark streaks or spots appear on top of the custard remove the tray from the oven.

Transfer the mixture to a blender, ensuring that you scrape out all of the brown pieces of custard from the sides of the pan. Add the gelatin to the hot custard and

blend on high speed for four minutes until a smooth cream forms. Pour 100 gms of the cream into a 16 cm round ring and freeze.

Pear jelly: Soften gelatin in 25 gms cold water. Blend the pear and the sugar syrup into a fine puree. Sieve. Place the puree and agar agar in a saucepan over medium heat. Bring to a boil and then remove from the heat. Add the gelatin and stir well to dissolve. Pour the jelly mix into small silicone flower molds.

Place the molds into the refrigerator and chill for one hour. Remove from the fridge and place into the freezer for one hour to harden the jellies and make them easier to extract. Keep frozen until needed.

Crumble: Place the ground hazelnuts, rice flour and the sugars into a large bowl and add the cold butter. Using fingertips rub the ingredients together until a fine sandy texture is formed. Add the chopped hazelnuts and mix to combine. Spread the crumb evenly and thinly on a baking tray lined with baking paper and bake at 140°C in a preheated oven for 30 minutes, or until toasted and light golden brown. Remove the tray from the oven and leave to cool.

Chocolate mousse: Soften gelatin in 25 gms cold water. Place cream (A), milk and honey in a small saucepan over medium heat and bring gently to scalding point. Place the egg yolks in a mixing bowl. Pour the scalded mixture onto the egg yolks while mixing thoroughly with a whisk.

Transfer the egg mixture to a medium saucepan over medium heat. Cook until the temperature reaches 85°C , ensuring the custard does not curdle. Pour the custard over the chocolate and set aside for one minute. Add the gelatin to the mixture and, mix well starting from the centre. Cool to 50°C. Gently fold the cream (B) until it is well incorporated. This should be used immediately.

Assembly: Line a round ring of 20 cm diameter with acetate strips. Using a palette knife, spread evenly 70 gms of chocolate and caramel spread on the brownie base. Place the frozen disc of pear cream on top and push down gently to make it stick. Spoon some caramelised pears evenly onto the pear cream.

Place the lined ring over this assembled brownie and ensure it is placed in the centre, leaving even space all around. Pour or pipe the chocolate mousse into the ring, ensuring it covers the assembled brownie completely and that it fills the gap between the ring and the brownie. Fill the ring to the top. Place the cake into the freezer. Remove cake from the ring. Sift cocoa powder over the cake. Pipe three mounds of caramel spread onto the top of the cake. Place pear jellies onto the side of the caramel spread and then spoon some crumble on the side of each jelly. Garnish with chocolate decorations.

RASPBERRY CRUMBLE CAKE

Yield – A 23 cm ring cake

Crumble
All-purpose flour – 150 gms
Almond powder – 60 gms
Brown sugar – 75 gms
Caster sugar – 75 gms
Unsalted butter,
cold – 125 gms
Rolled oats – 20 gms
Almonds, flaked – 25 gms

Cake
Unsalted butter, soft – 125 gms
Caster sugar – 275 gms
Zest of 1 lemon, grated
Vanilla extract – 1 tsp
Eggs – 3
All-purpose flour – 225 gms
Baking powder – ½ tsp
Baking soda – ¼ tsp
Milk – 125 ml
Raspberries – 125 gms

Crumble: Combine flour, almond powder and sugars in a large bowl. Rub in butter until mixture resembles fine breadcrumbs. Add cats and flaked almonds; press mixture together with your fingers to create large uneven lumps. Store in refrigerator.

Cake: Sift flour, baking powder and baking soda, and keep aside. Beat butter, sugar, rind and vanilla extract in the bowl of a stand mixer with paddle attachment until pale and fluffy. Beat in eggs, one at a time, until just combined. Add combined sifted dry ingredients and milk; beat on low speed until just combined. Increase speed to medium; beast for one minute or until mixture is smooth. Spoon mixture into a greased ring mold and smoothen the surface. Bake cake at 180°C in a preheated oven for 20 minutes.

Remove cake from oven and working quickly, scatter raspberries over cake, pushing them lightly into the mixture; sprinkle with crumble topping.

Bake cake a further 30 minutes or until a skewer inserted into the centre comes out clean. Stand cake in pan for 10 minutes before transferring to a wire rack to cool. Dust with icing sugar.

CARAMEL & CALVADOS CAKE

Yield – Two 23 cm round cakes

Chocolate sponge
Egg yolks – 8
Caster sugar – 110 gms
All-purpose flour – 85 gms
Cocoa powder – 20 gms
Almond flour – 125 gms
Unsalted butter, melted – 70 gms
Egg whites – 6
Caster sugar – 70 gms
Apples, sliced – 4
Calvados, to sprinkle

Caramel cream
Icing sugar – 185 gms
Cream 35% – 250 gms
Liquid glucose – 60 gms
Honey – 20 gms
Seeds of 1 Vanilla bean

Caramel mousse
Caramel cream – 120 gms (recipe on right)
Egg yolks – 2
Calvados – 50 gms
Gelatin powder – 12 gms
Cream, 35%, whipped – 600 gms

Calvados mousse
Eggs – 2
Egg yolks – 2
Caster sugar – 70 gms
Dark chocolate 60-70% – 190 gms
Gelatin powder – 8 gms
Calvados – 30 ml
Cream, 35%, whipped – 450 gms

Nappage
Liquid glucose – 160 gms
Dextrose – 300 gms
Water – 650 gms
Sugar – 420 gms
Citric acid powder – 2.5 gms
NH Pectin – 18 gms

Caramel glaze
Caramel cream – 140 gms (recipe on right)
Nappage – 300 gms (recipe on right)

Chocolate sponge: Beat the egg yolks and sugar to the ribbon stage. At the same time, sift all the dry ingredients and keep aside. Whip the whites to stiff peaks, adding the sugar little by little. Mix a small amount of the whipped whites to the yolk and sugar mixture. Fold the dry ingredients and the rest of the whipped whites. To finish, add the melted butter previously mixed with a little of the yolk and sugar mixture.

Divide the batter in four rings of 20 cm diameter. Put one sliced apple on top in each ring. Now bake at 170°C in a preheated oven for about 15-20 minutes. Sprinkle with calvados.

Caramel cream: Heat the cream and keep it aside. Melt the icing sugar until golden yellow and then pour the heated cream over it. Add glucose, honey and vanilla seeds Boil the ingredients together up to 103°C; on reaching this temperature immediately strain through a fine sieve into a stainless steel bowl. After it has cooled a little, cover the caramel cream with cling film and store in the refrigerator until needed.

Caramel mousse: Soften gelatin in 60 gms cold water. Whisk the caramel cream with the egg yolks until frothy and then stir in the melted gelatin mixed with Calvados into the tempered caramel cream and finally fold in the whipped cream. Divide and fill in the two silicone rings of 18 cm diameter immediately and place these into the freezer.

Calvados mousse: Soften gelatin in 40 gms cold water. Mix eggs and egg yolks with sugar and heat to 86°C while whisking all the time; pass through a fine sieve and whisk till cool. Melt the gelatin and mix Calvados and add to egg mix. Melt chocolate to 54°C, and add a small quantity of the whipped cream to lighten it. Now add chocolate to the above mixture and add the remaining whipped cream with a spatula. The combination should not lose air and should remain light. 263

Nappage: Mix water, glucose and dextrose and heat up to 40°C. Sprinkle pectin, previously mixed with sugar, with a whisk. Bring to boil for two minutes, add citric acid, and boil for one minute. Skim off the foam.

Caramel glaze: Temper the caramel cream to approximately 25°C and then stir in the nappage and warm a little.

Assembly: Line two gateau rings of 23 cm diameter with acetate strips as high as the ring. Place cocoa sponge with Calvados apples into it. Pour the Calvados chocolate mousse in the two rings on top of the sponges. Now insert the second set of sponges on top of the mousse. Once again cover each ring with mousse and freeze the assembled cake. To finish, remove the assembled chocolate cake and mousse from freezer and place caramel mousse on top.

Cover the surface of the cake with caramel glaze. Embellish with crushed meringue and streusel on the sides and decorate as desired.

CARAMEL & CALVADOS CAKE

ABSOLUTE COCONUT CAKE

Yield – A 23 cm round cake

Cake
All-purpose flour – 400 gms
Baking powder – 2 tsp
Salt – ½ tsp
Unsalted butter, soft – 250 gms
Icing sugar, sifted – 450 gms
Eggs, separated – 4
Vanilla extract – 10 ml
Milk – 350 ml
Coconut milk – 150 ml
Coconut, dried, shredded – 75 gms
Cream of tartar – ¼ tsp

Frosting
Egg whites – 4
Fleur de sel – a pinch
Caster sugar – 200 gms
Liquid glucose – 150 gms
Vanilla extract – 2 tsp

Decoration
Coconut, dried, shredded – 200 gms
Coconut, shavings, fresh

Cake: Butter the insides of three round 23 cm layer cake pans. Line the bottom of each pan with a circle of parchment paper.

Sift the flour, baking powder and salt and keep aside. Cream the butter in the bowl of a stand mixer with paddle attachment on medium speed for three minutes. Add the icing sugar in three batches, beating for one minute after each portion is added. Beat in the egg yolks, two at a time, mixing for 30 seconds after each addition. Blend in the vanilla extract. On low speed, add sifted flour in three batches, alternating with the milk in two batches, which means beginning with the sifted mixture followed by a portion of milk. Finally blend in the coconut.

In a clean mixing bowl whip the egg whites until foamy, add the cream of tartar, and continue beating until firm peaks are formed.

Stir about one-quarter of the whipped egg whites into the coconut batter, and then fold through the remaining whites.

Spoon the batter into the three prepared layer cake baking pans, dividing it evenly among them.

Bake at 180°C in a preheated oven for 30 minutes, or until risen and set. A skewer inserted in the centre of each layer should come out clean.

Cool the cake layers in the pans for 10 to 12 minutes. Invert the cakes on to cooling racks.

Frosting: Place the egg whites, salt, sugar and glucose in the bain-marie. Beat the frosting mixture for seven minutes until fluffy. Remove from the heat, and beat in the vanilla extract.

Assembly: Place a cake layer on the platter. Spread a little of the frosting on the cake layer and sprinkle with some of the shredded coconut. Place the second layer on top, spread with a little frosting, and top with some coconut. Carefully place the third layer on top. Frost the top and sides of the cake and generously coat the freshly frosted surface with the remaining coconut. Decorate with fresh coconut shavings.

BEET BERRY CAKE

Yield – A 26 cm round cake

Cake
Unsalted butter – 225 gms
Dark chocolate, 60-70%, melted – 125 gms
Brown sugar – 250 gms
Invert sugar – 20 gms
Eggs – 4
Fleur de sel – a pinch
All-purpose flour – 70 gms
Beetroot powder – 40 gms
Cocoa powder – 10 gms

Ganache
Cream, 35% – 125 gms
Dark chocolate, 60-70%, melted – 100gms
Invert sugar – 10 gms

Strawberry cream
Milk – 85 gms
Strawberry puree – 85 gms
Caster sugar – 10 gms
White chocolate – 50 gms
Iota carrageenan – 1 gm

Beetroot jelly
Strawberry puree – 200 gms
Water – 50 gms
Beetroot powder – 25 gms
Red wine vinegar – 25 gms
Caster sugar – 25 gms
Gelatin powder – 7 gms
Citric acid – 0.5 gms

Chocolate mousse
Strawberry puree – 150 gms
Caster sugar – 30 gms
Egg yolks – 25 gms
Gelatin powder – 5 gms
Dark chocolate 60-70% , melted – 195 gms
Cream, 35%, softly whipped – 270 gms

Beetroot shavings
White chocolate, tempered – 100 gms
Beetroot powder – 10 gms

Glaze
Water – 50 gms
Caster sugar – 125 gms
Glucose – 25 gms
Gelatin powder – 10 gms
Cocoa powder – 40 gms
Unsalted butter – 35 gms
Neutral nappage – 215 gms

Meringues
Egg whites – 2
Caster sugar – 100 gms
Icing sugar – 60 gms
Beetroot powder to sprinkle

Cake: Sift flour, cocoa powder and beetroot powder and keep aside. Mix butter with salt and sugars in a bowl of a stand mixer with a paddle attachment and beat on medium speed till well mixed. Add melted chocolate and mix again. Add eggs one at a time and mix. Fold in the sifted flour. Pour in a lined 23 cm cake ring and bake at 200°C in a preheated oven for 15 minutes. Cool and transfer to a clean cake ring of 23 cm.

Ganache: Heat the cream with invert sugar and pour over the melted chocolate. Mix with a hand blender. Pour over the cake in the ring and freeze.

Strawberry cream: Dissolve the Iota-carrageenan with the sugar and add to the puree and mix. Bring to a boil. Add milk and boil again. Pour over the chocolate and emulsify with a hand blender. Spread over the ganache in the cake ring and re-freeze.

Beetroot jelly: Soften gelatin in 35 gms cold water. Melt and mix all the ingredients in a jug using a hand blender. Pour in a bowl of a stand mixer with whisk attachment and whip till foamy. Spread on top of the strawberry cream and re-freeze.

Chocolate mousse: Soften gelatin in 25 gms cold water. Heat the strawberry purée and the sugar together. Pour onto the egg yolks and cook to 85°C. Add hydrated gelatin and mix. Pour the mixture over the melted chocolate and emulsify with a hand blender. Fold in the cream with a rubber spatula. Put most of the mousse in a 26 cm lined cake ring; then put the frozen assembly (as above), with the cake side up. Cover with mousse to level the ring and freeze again.

Beetroot shavings: Mix chocolate and beetroot powder. Spread onto a marble surface. With a knife at an angle scrape the almost hardened mix to make shavings. Set aside.

Glaze: Soften gelatin in 50 gms cold water and keep aside. Boil the water with the glucose and sugar. Dissolve the hydrated gelatin in the sugar mixture. Add the cocoa powder, butter and neutral nappage. Strain and set aside. Use at 35°C.

Meringues: Whisk the egg whites until frothy. Add caster sugar little at a time, whisking continuously until smooth, shiny and stiff peaks are formed. Gently fold in the icing sugar with a spatula. Transfer to a pastry bag fitted with a small round tip. Pipe small mounds on a parchment lined tray. Sprinkle with beetroot powder. Bake at 90°C for one hour and then remove from oven and leave to cool.

Assembly: Remove the assembly from the freezer. Demold and cover with glaze. Decorate with small meringues and chocolate decorations and place beetroot shavings along the lower edge of the cake.

HOT PEPPER CAKE

Yield – A 20 cm round cake

Cake
All-purpose flour – 250 gms
Cocoa powder – 65 gms
Dark chocolate 60-70%, melted – 100 gms
Baking powder – 1 tsp
Fleur de sel – 1 tsp
Brown sugar – 350 gms
Eggs – 3
Extra virgin olive oil – 250 ml
Tabasco/hot pepper sauce – 2 tsp
Vanilla extract – 1 tsp
Cocoa powder and flour – for dusting

Ganache
Dark chocolate 60-70%, chopped – 350 gms
Cream 35% – 175 gms
Unsalted butter – 25 gms
Light brown sugar – 20 gms
Tabasco – a few drops

Garnish
Red chilli – 1
Caster sugar – 30 gms

Cake: Mix together two teaspoons each of all-purpose flour and cocoa and use to dust the inside of the lined cake pan, tapping out the excess. In a large bowl sift together the flour, cocoa powder, baking powder and salt. Add the sugar, eggs, olive oil, Tabasco/hot pepper sauce, vanilla, melted chocolate and 250 ml water. Mix thoroughly until blended. Pour into the prepared cake pan and bake at 130°C in a preheated oven for 45 minutes, until the top is no longer shiny and has formed a light crust. (The inside should still be slightly soft). Let the cake cool for 15 minutes before removing from the pan and transferring to a wire rack.

Ganache: Heat the cream, butter, brown sugar and a few drops of Tabasco in a small pan until boiling, stir until smooth, then pour over the chocolate. Leave for two minutes and then stir until smooth. Leave to cool until it thickens slightly.

Garnish: In the meanwhile, thinly slice the chilli and roll in the sugar. Place the chilli slices on the lined baking sheet and bake at 140°C in a preheated oven for 5-10 minutes or until the sugar begins to crystallize. Once this has happened, place the chill slices back in the sugar to add even more crunch. Place the cooled cake on a serving plate and coat the top and sides with the ganache. Decorate with the candied chillies.

GLACE FRUIT CAKE

Yield – A 23 x 10 cm loaf

Raisins – 100 gms
Dark rum – 100 ml
Unsalted butter, soft – 125 gms
Icing sugar – 125 gms
Eggs – 2
Egg yolk – 1
Seeds of 1 Vanilla bean
All-purpose flour – 190 gms
Baking powder – 1 tsp
Glace cherries – 100 gms
Glace fruits, mixed – 100 gms
Apricot jam, warmed, sieved – 75 gms
Glace fruits, to decorate – 50 gms

Soak the raisins in 50 ml rum for 15 minutes. Whisk the butter and icing sugar together in a large bowl for one minute. Beat in the whole eggs one at a time, followed by the egg yolk. Scrape the vanilla seeds into the mixture and mix until evenly combined. Sift about four-fifths of the flour with the baking powder over the mixture and fold in carefully.

Toss the raisins, glace cherries and other glace fruits with the remaining flour. Fold in the cake mixture into the tin and spread evenly. Bake at 200°C in a preheated oven for 5 minutes, then lower the setting to 180°C, and cook for a further 30-40 minutes, or until a skewer inserted into the centre comes out clean.

On removing the cake from the oven, sprinkle with remaining rum over the surface. Leave in the tin for 10-15 minutes then remove and transfer to a wire rack to cool. Lightly brush the surface of the cake with the warmed apricot jam, and then arrange glace fruits over the top to decorate.

MARBLE VELVET CAKE

Yield – A 26 cm ring cake

Cake
Dark chocolate 60-70%, melted – 85 gms
Egg yolks – 6
Sour cream – 240 gms
Vanilla extract – 2 tsp
All-purpose flour – 300 gms
Caster sugar – 300 gms
Baking powder – 1 tsp
Baking soda – ½ tsp
Fleur de sel – ½ tsp
Unsalted butter, melted – 250 gms

Glaze
Dark chocolate 60-70%, chopped – 115 gms
Cream 35% – 75 gms
Liquid glucose – 20 gms
French brandy – 1 tsp

Cake: Butter and flour the ring pan and keep ready. In a medium bowl, whisk the yolks, 60 gms of the sour cream, and the vanilla just until lightly combined. In the bowl of a stand mixer fitted with the paddle attachment, mix the flour, sugar, baking powder, baking soda, and salt on low speed for 30 seconds. Add the butter and the remaining sour cream. Mix on low speed until the dry ingredients are moistened. Raise the speed to medium and beat for two minutes while scraping down the sides of the bowl.

Starting on medium-low speed, gradually add the egg mixture in three parts. After each addition, beat on medium speed for 20 seconds each time so that all the ingredients are well incorporated. Remove almost one-third of the batter to a bowl and stir in the melted chocolate until uniform in colour. Put the chocolate and plain batter together in the ring pan in alternate batches. Use a skewer or butter knife to marblize the batter lightly. Bake at 170°C in a preheated oven for about one hour, or until a skewer inserted between the tube and the side comes out clean and the cake springs back when pressed lightly in the centre. Cool and unmold the cake and invert on a wire rack for 10 minutes.

Glaze: Heat the cream and glucose to a boiling point and pour it over the chocolate. Cover the bowl for 5 minutes to allow the chocolate to melt. Gently stir together the chocolate and cream until smooth, trying not to create air bubbles. Press the mixture through the strainer, stir in the brandy and cool until tepid.

Set the cake on a serving plate. Pour the glaze evenly over the top of the cake, allowing it to drip down the sides. Decorate, as desired.

MINTY RASPBERRY CAKE

Yield – A 23 x 10 cm loaf

Cake
Icing sugar – 90 gms
Caster sugar – 90 gms
Eggs – 3
Cream 35% – 80 gms
All-purpose flour – 180 gms
Almond powder – 40 gms
Unsalted butter – 140 gms
Fleur de sel – a pinch
Baking powder – ½ tsp
Red colour, as desired

Butter cream
Unsalted butter, soft – 400 gms
Icing sugar – 200 gms
Mint leaves – 1 cup

Raspberry syrup
Sugar – 90 gms
Water – 300 gms
Raspberry puree – 100 gms

Raspberry jam
Raspberry puree – 240 gms
Raspberries, frozen – 60 gms
Caster sugar – 150 gms
Pectin NH – 9 gms
Citric acid – 3 gms

Topping
Mint jelly cubes
Mint sprigs
Edible flowers
Raspberry liqueur

Cake: Mix icing sugar, caster sugar and butter in the bowl of a stand mixer with paddle attachment till light and fluffy. Add eggs gradually, making an emulsion. Sift the flour and baking powder. Add in together with almond powder and salt. Add coloring as desired. Fold in the cream. Pour in greased and parchment lined mold. Bake cake at 165°C in a preheated oven for 30-40 minutes. Cool for five minutes, then remove from tin and cool completely on a wire rack.

Butter cream: Boil 100 ml water. Add mint leaves for 10 seconds. Remove with a sieve and place directly on iced water. Strain and add 100 ml water and mix in blender. Strain and use 90 gms. Whip butter and sugar with whisk attachment in the bowl of a stand mixer. Add the warm mint water to lighten the mixture. Use blowtorch on outside of the bowl, to make a proper emulsion.

Raspberry syrup: Boil sugar and water. Cool and stir in the raspberry puree.

Raspberry jam: Mix pectin and sugar together. Heat puree and raspberries in a pan to 40°C. Add pectin and sugar mix gradually while whisking, and bring to a boil. Add citric acid and reserve in refrigerator, covered with cling film.

Assembly: Slice cake into half horizontally. Sprinkle with syrup on both the sides and spread raspberry jam on the first layer. Cover with second layer, with the cut side facing the top. Pipe mint butter cream on top. Decorate with mint jelly cubes, mint leaves and edible flowers. Add a few pipettes filled with raspberry liqueur.

CHOCO BERRY CAKE

Yield – A 23 cm round cake

Streusel
Unsalted butter, cold, cubed – 50 gms
Brown sugar – 50 gms
All-purpose flour – 50 gms
Coriander seeds, crushed – 10 gms
Almond flour – 50 gms

Sacher sponge
Almond paste, chopped – 140 gms
Egg yolks – 4
Egg – 1
All-purpose flour – 30 gms
Cocoa powder – 15 gms
Dark chocolate, 60-70% – 35 gms
Unsalted butter – 30 gms
Egg whites – 2
Caster sugar – 45 gms

Custard
Cream – 500 gms
Milk – 500 gms
Egg yolks – 10
Caster sugar – 400 gms

Chocolate cremeux
Custard – 300 gms
(recipe on next page)
Dark chocolate, 60-70% – 150 gms

Raspberry gel
Raspberry puree – 150 gms
Neutral glaze – 125 gms

Chocolate mousse
Custard – 225 gms
(recipe on next page)
Dark chocolate, 60-70% – 320 gms
Cream 35%, soflty whipped – 400 gms

Whipped chocolate ganache
Cream, 35% (A) – 110 gms
Invert sugar – 15 gms
Liquid glucose – 15 gms
Dark chocolate, 60-70% – 100 gms
Cream, 35% (B), cold – 240 gms

Shiny chocolate glaze
Caster sugar – 360 gms
Cocoa powder – 120 gms
Water – 280 gms
Cream, 35% – 210 gms
Gelatin powder – 22 gms

Streusel: Mix butter with other ingredients and blend in a stand mixer with the paddle attachment. Stop mixing when the dough comes together, and chill for a minimum of 30 minutes. Push the cold dough through a 4 mm grill to obtain regular-sized pieces. Store in the refrigerator.

Sacher sponge: Sift flour and cocoa powder and set aside. Soften almond paste in microwave for 20 seconds. Beat the almond paste with egg yolks until creamy. Add the whole egg and whisk until the mixture reaches ribbon stage. Melt chocolate and butter to 50°C. Beat egg whites, gradually add the sugar, until the mixture holds soft peaks. Stir a large spoonful into the melted chocolate and butter until mixed in. Pour the melted chocolate mixture into the rest of the whisked egg whites and carefully fold in until evenly combined. Add the almond paste and egg mix, followed by the flour and cocoa powder, and fold everything together.

Pour the batter into the cake ring of 20 cm diameter. Sprinkle with pieces of raw streusel and bake at 180°C in a preheated oven for about 20-25 minutes.

Custard: Mix the egg yolks with sugar. Bring the cream and milk to a boil and pour onto the egg yolks. Cook until the mixture reaches 84°C. Strain and use immediately.

Chocolate cremeux: Make an emulsion by slowly pouring 300 gms custard onto the melted chocolate, until smooth, glossy and elastic. Blend to perfect the emulsion, taking care not to incorporate any air while working at 35-45°C.

Raspberry gel: Blend the raspberry pulp with the glaze. Set aside.

Chocolate mousse: Make an emulsion by slowly pouring 225 gms of hot custard onto the melted chocolate until smooth, glossy and elastic. Mix with a hand blender and cool to 35-40°C. Stabilize by adding a little whipped cream. As soon as the mixture is smooth, add the remaining whipped cream and use immediately.

Whipped chocolate ganache: Bring the cream (A) to a boil with the glucose and invert sugar. Slowly pour the boiling liquid onto the chocolate and stir in the centre to create an elastic texture with a glossy appearance. Add the cold cream (B) and mix with hand blender. Set aside in the refrigerator for 2-3 hours or overnight if possible. Remove from refrigerator and beat the ganache in a bowl of a stand mixer with whisk attachment till it is soft but firm enough to pipe.

Shiny chocolate glaze: Soften gelatin in 110 gms cold water. Mix sugar and cocoa powder. Make a well in the centre and add the water, stirring constantly to make a paste. Put the paste in a large, heavy-based saucepan and add the cream. Place the pan over medium heat and, stirring constantly, bring the mixture to a boil for three minutes to ensure that the cocoa powder has been sufficiently cooked. Remove the pan from the heat. Add the gelatin and stir well to dissolve. Strain the hot mixture through a sieve into a clean plastic container. Store the glaze in the refrigerator until needed. To use, melt the glaze in the microwave in short, high bursts until fluid. Mix with hand blender and use at 35°C.

Assembly: Cut a disc of Sacher cake, and pipe some small mounds of chocolate cremeux on top. Now fill the gaps between the mounds with raspberry gel and freeze. Place frozen assembly in a ring of 23 cm lined with acetate, and fill and level with chocolate mousse and again freeze.

Cover the cake with glaze. Pipe the whipped ganache in a lattice pattern with a plain tip. Decorate as desired.

MATCHA ALMOND CAKE

Yield – A 35 x 7 cm loaf

Matcha cake
Eggs – 3
Egg yolks – 2
Caster sugar (A) – 90 gms
Egg whites – 3
Caster sugar (B) – 35 gms
Unsalted butter, melted – 15 gms
Milk – 15 gms
All-purpose flour – 25 gms
Cornflour – 6 gms
Matcha green tea – 15 gms

Crème anglaise
Cream, 35% – 500 gms
Egg yolks – 5
Caster sugar – 50 gms

Raspberry cremeux
Crème anglaise – 125 gms (recipe on right)
Invert sugar – 25 gms
Raspberry puree – 125 gms
Dark chocolate, 60-70% – 100 gms

Praline cremeux
Almond praline – 75 gms
Crème anglaise – 250 gms (recipe on right)
Gelatin powder – 2 gms

Green tea cremeux
Crème anglaise – 250 gms (recipe on right)
Gelatin powder – 3 gms
Matcha green tea – 4 gms
Cream, 35%, softly whipped – 25 gms

Almond mousse
Milk – 130 gms
Gelatin powder – 5 gms
White chocolate – 250 gms
Marzipan – 65 gms
Cream, 35%, softly whipped – 260 gms

Topping
Neutral glaze
Gooseberries

Matcha cake: Sift flour, cornflour and matcha tea; keep aside. Heat milk and butter together, again keep aside. Heat the eggs, egg yolks and sugar (A), whisking continuously over a bain-marie till light and fluffy. Prepare a meringue with the egg whites and add sugar (B) gradually and using a rubber spatula fold the egg and sugar mixture in. Now fold in the butter and milk mixture and finish with the sifted flours. Spread on a baking sheet. Bake cake at 200°C, in a preheated oven, for 12 minutes. Cut to fit inside a rectangular mold.

Crème anglaise: Warm the cream to 50°C and pour over the egg yolks that have been already beaten with the sugar. Cook to 85°C and keep hot and ready to use in the three cremeux.

Raspberry cremeux: Add the invert sugar to the hot crème anglaise then, little by little, pour over the chocolate and emulsify with a hand blender. Finish by adding the raspberry puree. Cover with cling wrap and cool in refrigerator.

Praline cremeux: Soften gelatin in 10 gms cold water. Add to hot crème anglaise and mix. Emulsify the praline, gradually pouring the still-hot crème anglaise and blend with hand blender. Cover with cling wrap and cool in refrigerator.

Green tea cremeux: Soften gelatin in 15 gms cold water. Add to hot crème anglaise and mix. Cool rapidly to 30°C and add the Matcha green tea powder, and whipped cream. Mix with spatula and cover with cling wrap and cool in refrigerator.

Almond mousse: Soften gelatin in 25 gms cold water. Boil the milk and add the gelatin. Pour over chocolate and mix. Add the marzipan and mix with hand blender. Cool to 35°C and fold in whipped cream.

Assembly: Pour the almond mousse into the frame on top of the sponge and freeze. Pipe the different cremeux onto the mousse using a plain tip and freeze.

Topping: Prepare the glaze by adding 20% water to the neutral glaze and boil and spray at 70°C over the frozen assembly. Decorate with gooseberries.

INDULGENT CHOCOLATE CAKE

Yield – A 20 cm round cake

Cake
All-purpose flour – 250 gms
Cocoa powder – 50 gms
Instant coffee powder – 2 tsp
Fleur de sel – ¼ tsp
Baking soda – 1 tsp
Eggs – 3
Caster sugar – 250 gms
Brewed coffee, at room temperature – 250 gms

Chocolate hazelnut spread
Hazelnut praline – 600 gms
Hazelnut paste – 300 gms
Milk chocolate, melted – 330 gms
Milk powder – 75 gms
Unsalted butter – 20 gms
Grape seed oil – 30 gms
Fleur de sel – 1 gms

Mascarpone filling
Chocolate-hazelnut spread– 750 gms (recipe below)
Mascarpone cheese – 280 gms

Decoration
Pistachios
Dried rose petals
Cocoa nibs, roasted

Cake: Line two 20 cm round cake pans with parchment paper and lightly coat with non-stick cooking spray. Sift flour, cocoa, coffee, salt and baking soda together in a bowl. Put the eggs, sugar and brewed coffee in the bowl of stand mixer with whisk attachment, and whisk until thickened and light in colour. Gradually whisk in dry ingredients until smooth.

Divide the batter evenly between the two cake pans and bake at 180°C in a preheated oven for 20 minutes or until a skewer inserted into the centre of the cake comes out clean. Transfer cake pans to a cooling rack and let cool for five minutes. Gently invert and cool to room temperature.

Chocolate hazelnut spread: Mix praline with the hazelnut paste. Add the milk powder, butter, salt and chocolate. Lastly, add oil and mix with hand blender.

Mascarpone filling: In a large bowl, fold the spread and mascarpone together until smooth. Cover and refrigerate until ready to use. If needed, stir the filling to soften before using.

Assembly: On one chocolate cake layer pipe a thick layer of the chocolate-mascarpone filling, starting at the edge of the cake and working to the centre. Scatter the top of the filling generously with the chopped pistachios. Gently place the second layer of cake on top of the filling. Pipe the remaining filling on top of the cake, swirling into a decorative pattern, and sprinkle with pistachios, rose petals and cocoa nibs.

MOCHA CAKE

Yield – A 23 cm round cake

Cake
Egg – 1
Caster sugar – 30 gms
Almonds, ground – 30 gms
All-purpose flour – 10 gms
Baking powder – ¼ tsp
Unsalted butter, melted – 15 gms

Coffee syrup
Water – 90 gms
Sugar – 25 gms
Coffee beans, roasted – 20 gms
Instant coffee – 1 tsp

Coffee & tonka cremeux
Caster sugar – 40 gms
Liquid glucose – 5 gms
Cream, 35% – 100 gms
Tonka beans, grated – 1.5 gms
Gelatin powder – 4 gms
Cocoa butter, melted – 7.5 gms
Milk chocolate – 40 gms

Vanilla cremeux
Mascarpone – 40 gms
Cream 35% – 85 gms
Seeds of ½ Vanilla bean
Gelatin powder – 2 gms

Coffee Bavarian cream
Milk – 200 gms
Egg yolks – 2
Caster sugar – 40 gms
Gelatin powder – 8 gms
Coffee beans, chopped – 20 gms
Instant coffee – 5 gms
Cream, 35%, softly whipped – 325 gms

Coffee glaze
Water – 150 gms
Caster sugar – 65 gms
Iota Carrageenan – 2.5 gms
Sorbitol – 10 gms
Liquid glucose – 100 gms
Invert sugar – 25 gms
Cream, 35% – 50 gms
Gelatin powder – 10 gms
White chocolate – 150 gms
Instant coffee – 5 gms

Cake: Whisk the egg and sugar to a ribbon stage. Add the sifted ground almonds, flour and baking powder and then the melted butter. Pour into a ring of 20 cm diameter and bake at 190°C in a preheated oven for eight minutes.

Coffee syrup: Pour boiling water over the chopped coffee beans and add the instant coffee. Make a pale caramel with the sugar. Deglaze the caramel with the coffee water. Drain and cool. Brush over the cooled sponge.

Coffee and tonka cremeux: Soften gelatin in 20 gms of cold water. Bring the cream to boil and infuse tonka beans. Make a pale caramel with the sugar and glucose. Deglaze with the warm cream. Add the gelatin and the cocoa butter and strain. Pour onto the milk chocolate. Blend, cool and spread onto the soaked biscuit sponge, which is in a 20 cm ring, lined with acetate.

Vanilla cremeux: Soften gelatin in 10 gms of cold water. Heat cream, sugar, and vanilla seeds add gelatin and mix. Whip the mascarpone and then combine the two mixtures. Pour on top of the coffee/tonka cremeux and cake and freeze.

Coffee Bavarian cream: Soften gelatin in 40 gms cold water. Infuse the milk with the coffee beans for 30 minutes, strain and heat with instant coffee. Mix with beaten egg yolks and sugar. Again heat the whole lot to 82°C, stirring continuously. Add the gelatin. Leave to cool. Fold in the whipped cream.

Coffee glaze: Soften gelatin in 50 gms cold water. Heat the water and add the iota that has been mixed with half the sugar. Bring to boil and add the sorbitol, glucose and invert sugar. Then add the gelatin, cream and remaining sugar. Mix with a hand blender. Pour onto the chocolate. Blend and add the instant coffee. Strain and cover with cling film and refrigerate.

Assembly: Pour 300 gms of coffee Bavarian cream into the 23 cm ring lined with acetate. Add the frozen assembly, vanilla cremeux side facing down. Pour some more Bavarian cream on top and smooth. When frozen, remove from the molds, invert and glaze with the coffee glaze at 40°C. Decorate as desired.

MOCHA CAKE

PINEAPPLE AND SAGE CAKE

Yield – A 23 cm round cake

Cake
Pineapple puree – 185 gms
Water – 60 gms
Caster sugar – 100 gms
Dry egg white
powder – 20 gms
Egg yolks – 2
Unsalted butter,
melted – 50 gms
All-purpose flour – 90 gms
Baking powder – 2 gms
Almond powder – 90 gms
Pineapple, pan-fried– 150 gms

Short crust
White chocolate,
melted – 45 gms
Unsalted butter, soft – 75 gms
Brown sugar – 15 gms
Almond flour – 30 gms
Egg yolk – 1
Fleur de sel – a pinch
All-purpose flour – 40 gms

Pineapple and sage layer
Gelatin powder – 3 gms
Pineapple, finely
diced – 40 gms
Agave syrup – 25 gms
Pineapple puree – 125 gms
Sage, fresh, chopped – 5 gms
White rum – 25 ml

Italian meringue
Egg whites – 2
Sugar – 115 gms
Water – 30 gms

Pineapple mousse
Italian meringue – 80 gms
(recipe on right)
Pineapple puree – 300 gms
Fresh sage – 5 gms
Gelatin powder – 7 gms
Cream 35%, softly
whipped – 120 gms

White glaze
Gelatin powder – 4 gms
Water – 30 ml
Caster sugar – 60 gms
Liquid glucose – 60 gms
Sweetened condensed
milk – 40 gms
White chocolate – 60 gms

Green sand
Pistachio chopped – 100 gms
Coconut, shredded – 200 gms
Matcha tea – 2 gms

Cake: Sieve flour and baking powder and set aside. Whisk pineapple puree, water, sugar and egg white powder to a soft peak stage. Add yolks, one by one and mix gently. Fold the flour and almond powder. Finally, add melted butter and mix gently. Pour on a parchment-lined tray and spread the pan-fried pineapple on top. Bake sponge at 200°C in a preheated oven, for 8-10 minutes. Cool on a wire rack. Cut into a 20 cm round.

Short crust: Whisk the butter and brown sugar until pale, stir in the almond flour, egg yolk, and salt and then fold in the flour. Stir in the melted chocolate, mix well and pour into 20 cm ring and bake at 150°C in a preheated oven until lightly browned. Cool in the ring.

Pineapple and sage layer: Soften the gelatin in 20 gms cold water. Pan-fry the diced pineapple with the agave syrup without caramelizing. Stir in the pineapple puree and sage and heat to 60°C, strain through a sieve, pressing down to extract all the juice. Stir in the rum. Add gelatin and stir till dissolved. Pour into the 20 cm ring and freeze.

Italian meringue: Heat water and sugar to 118°C. Pour over egg whites and whisk till it cools to 30°C.

Pineapple mousse: Infuse sage in pineapple puree for 2-3 hours in the refrigerator. Strain and mix gelatin in one third of the puree and keep for 20 minutes. Heat to 45°C and mix in rest of the puree. Leave in refrigerator till it starts to gel. Fold in the Italian meringue and cream and use immediately.

White glaze: Soften gelatin in 20 gms cold water. In a saucepan, heat the water, sugar, and glucose to 102°C. Stir in the condensed milk and gelatin and stir in, then pour over the chocolate and mix with the hand blender. Store in the refrigerator overnight. Use at 35°C.

Green sand: Mix all the ingredients and keep aside.

Assembly: Lay the sponge cake in 23 cm ring and spread some of the pineapple mousse over it in a smooth layer. Carefully put the frozen pineapple and sage layer in the centre and cover with another layer of mousse. Top with the short crust and spread with more mousse. Freeze for one hour. Carefully remove the ring and place the assembled cake on a rack over a baking sheet. Smooth the mousse with a spatula before pouring over the white glaze. Put the green sand on the bottom edges of the cake. Decorate as desired.

PINEAPPLE AND SAGE CAKE

DARK SECRET BERRY CAKE

Yield – Two 23 cm ring cakes

Dacquoise
Almond powder – 140 gms
Icing sugar – 180 gms
All-purpose flour – 20 gms
Cocoa powder – 20 gms
Sugar – 135 gms
Sea salt – 1.5 gms
Egg whites – 7

Sable
Unsalted butter – 35 gms
Icing sugar – 35 gms
Fleur de sel – a pinch
Egg – ½
Vanilla extract – ½ tsp
All-purpose flour – 50 gms
Almond powder – 15 gms
Almonds, chopped – 25 gms

Raspberry and black currant compote
Frozen raspberries – 70 gms
Raspberry puree – 200 gms
Black currant puree – 80 gms
Cloves, ground – ¼ tsp
Caster sugar – 40 gms
Pectin NH – 1 gm
Gelatin powder – 5 gms

Dark chocolate mousse
Cream, 35% (A) – 75 gms
Milk – 110 gms
Honey – 15 gms
Dark chocolate, 60-70% – 230 gms
Gelatin powder – 3 gms
Cream, 35% (B), softly whipped – 375 gms

Neutral nappage
Liquid glucose – 160 gms
Dextrose – 300 gms
Water – 660 gms
Caster sugar – 415 gms
Citric acid powder – 2.5 gms
NH Pectin – 17 gms

Dark cocoa glaze
Liquid glucose – 20 gms
Dextrose – 60 gms
Water – 20 gms
Cream, 35% – 90 gms
Caster sugar – 175 gms
Cocoa powder – 70 gms
Skimmed milk powder – 10 gms
Gelatin powder – 14 gms
Neutral nappage – 200 gms (recipe on right)

Dacquoise: Sift the almond powder, icing sugar, all-purpose flour and cocoa powder together. Make a meringue with the egg whites, sea salt, and sugar. Fold the flour mixture into the meringue. Spread the mixture into a 3 cm high frame and bake at 175°C in a preheated oven. Cool and cut four pieces to fit inside the 23 cm ring molds.

Sable: Cream the butter, icing sugar and salt together. Slowly add the vanilla and egg to the mixture. Sift the flour and almond powder together and add the dry ingredients to the butter mixture until it is combined. Cool the dough. Roll the sable out and cut two pieces to fit inside the ring molds. Press chopped almonds onto the sable and bake at 170°C. Bake the rest of the crumble and use for decoration.

Raspberry and black currant compote: Soften gelatin powder in 25 gms cold water. Heat the raspberries, black currant puree, raspberry puree and cloves. Mix the sugar and pectin NH together and add to the purees at 40°C. Bring the puree to a boil. Add the gelatin, and divide into the insert of the ring mold and freeze.

Dark chocolate mousse: Soften gelatin in 15 gms cold water. Boil cream (A) and milk. Add the gelatin to the warm cream to dissolve. Pour warm cream and gelatin over the chocolate and honey and make an emulsion with hand blender. At 40°C, fold the whipped cream (B) into the ganache.

Neutral nappage: Mix water, glucose and dextrose and heat up to 40°C. Sprinkle pectin, previously mixed with sugar, with a whisk. Bring to boil two minutes, add citric acid, and boil for one minute. Skim off the foam.

Dark cocoa glaze: Soften gelatin in 70 gms cold water. Mix glucose, dextrose, water, cream add sugar and heat to 103°C. Add cocoa powder and milk powder and bring to boil again. Strain the mixture, add the gelatin and neutral nappage and mix with hand blender. Refrigerate overnight and use at 35°C.

Assembly: Fill a ring mold halfway with the dark chocolate mousse. Place a dacquoise along with raspberry and black currant compote into the mousse. Place more mousse on top of the compote. Now set another dacquoise on top of the mousse. Spread yet another thin layer of mousse onto the dacquoise and place the almond sable on top. Freeze the assembly. Glaze the cake and put some crumbled sable on the sides.

DARK SECRET BERRY CAKE

PERSIMMON UPSIDE DOWN CAKE

Yield – A 26 cm round cake

Honey – 125 ml
Maple syrup – 125 ml
Unsalted butter, soft – 220 gms
Persimmons, sliced thinly – 600 gms
Caster sugar – 330 gms
Finely grated rind of 1 lemon
Eggs, separated – 3
Vanilla extract – 1 tsp
All-purpose flour – 115 gms
Baking powder – 1½ tsp
Milk – 180 ml
Fine semolina – 270 gms
Pistachios, chopped – 100 gms

For topping
Persimmons
Mint sprigs

Stir honey, maple syrup and 75 gms of the butter in a small saucepan over low heat for two minutes, or until butter melts. Increase heat to medium and bring to a boil. Boil for four minutes or until mixture thickens; and then cool for about five minutes. Pour half the maple syrup mixture over base of greased and parchment lined cake pan; arrange persimmon slices on base, positioning them slightly along the side of the pan.

Beat remaining butter with sugar and rind in the bowl of a stand mixer with a paddle attachment, until pale and fluffy. Beat in egg yolks and vanilla extract until combined. Add sifted flour and baking powder, and milk; beat on low speed until almost combined. Add semolina; beat until well combined. Beat egg whites in another bowl with whisk attachment, until firm peaks form; gently fold into cake mixture. Carefully spread mixture evenly over persimmon; scatter with pistachios.

Bake at 170°C in a preheated oven until a skewer inserted into the centre comes out clean. Stand cake in pan for 30 minutes. Run a palette knife around the edge of the cake, to loosen the cake from the pan and then turn out onto serving plate.

Top the cake with reserved maple syrup. Decorate with mint sprigs and roses made from persimmon thinly sliced.

VERY BLACK FOREST CAKE

Yield – Two 35 x 7 cm loaves

Chocolate sponge
Marzipan – 115 gms
Caster sugar (A) – 25 gms
Eggs – 2
Egg yolks – 5
All-purpose flour – 55 gms
Cocoa powder – 40 gms
Baking powder – 1 tsp
Unsalted butter, melted – 40 gms
Egg whites – 5
Caster sugar (B) – 100 gms

Macerated cherries
Morello cherries, with juice – 650 gms
Caster sugar – 110 gms
Kirsch – 75 gms
Morello cherry puree – 75 gms

Cherry compote
Macerated Morello cherry juice – 450 gms (recipe on right)
NH pectin – 10 gms
Caster sugar (A) – 30 gms
Caster sugar (B) – 30 gms
Citric acid solution – 2.5 gms
Gelatin powder – 10 gms

Creamy dark chocolate
Milk – 150 gms
Chocolate 60-70%, melted – 190 gms
Liquid glucose – 75 gms
Gelatin powder – 4 gms
Cream 35% – 300 gms

Vanilla cream
Cream 35% – 550 gms
Vanilla extract – 1 tsp
Liquid glucose – 55 gms
White chocolate – 370 gms
Gelatin powder – 15 gms
Kirsch – 55 gms
Cream 35%, softly whipped – 875 gms

Cream for topping
Cream 35% – 125 gms
Mascarpone cheese – 125 gms
Caster sugar – 20 gms
Vanilla extract – 1 tsp

Dark chocolate glaze
Liquid glucose – 40 gms
Dextrose – 120 gms
Water – 40 gms
Cream 35% – 180 gms
Caster sugar – 350 gms
Cocoa powder – 140 gms
Milk powder – 20 gms
Gelatin powder – 28 gms
Neutral nappage – 400 gms

Cocoa nib crunchy
Hazelnuts, toasted – 40 gms
Caster sugar – 75 gms
Unsalted butter – 60 gms
Liquid glucose – 25 gms
Milk – 20 gms
Cocoa nibs – 40 gms
Cocoa powder – 7 gms

Beetroot glass
Beetroot, cooked – 150 gms
Icing sugar – 20 gms
Isomalt – 25 gms
Liquid glucose – 5 gms

Chocolate sponge: Sieve flour, cocoa and baking powder and set aside. Blend the marzipan with the sugar (A) and gradually add the eggs and egg yolks. Add the dry ingredients then the melted butter. Beat the egg whites with sugar (B) and fold in the above mix. Pour into a baking sheet and bake at 200°C in a preheated oven for 15 minutes.

Macerated cherries: Take the juice from the can of the cherries and heat it with the sugar and Morello cherry puree. Add the Kirsch and macerate with the Morello cherries overnight.

Cherry compote: Soften the gelatin in 50 gms cold water. Mix pectin with sugar (A). Drain the Morello cherries (from above), reserving the juice. Heat the Morello cherry juice to 40°C then add the pectin NH and sugar. Bring to the boil, add the sugar (B) then add the citric acid solution and gelatin. Add the drained Morello cherries.

Creamy dark chocolate: Soften gelatin in 20 gms cold water. Bring the milk to the boil and pour onto the melted chocolate and glucose. Add the melted gelatin, then the cream. Mix with hand blender.

Vanilla cream: Soften gelatin in 75 gms cold water. Mix cream with the vanilla. Add the glucose and bring to the boil. Pour onto the white chocolate. Add the melted gelatin and the Kirsch. Mix with hand blender. Cool to 28°C and add the whipped cream.

Cream for topping: Whisk all ingredients together.

Dark chocolate glaze: Soften gelatin in 140 gms cold water. Mix glucose, dextrose, water, cream and sugar and bring to boil to 103°C-104°C. Stir with a whisk continuously. Add cocoa powder and milk powder and bring to boil again. Remove into a jug, add the gelatin and neutral nappage and mix with the hand blender. Strain and cover with cling film and refrigerate. Use at 35°C on the frozen cake.

Cocoa nib crunchy: Chop the hazelnuts. Combine the sugar, butter, glucose and milk in a saucepan and stir over medium-high heat until the mixture reaches 110°C. Remove from the heat and stir in the hazelnuts, cocoa nibs, and cocoa powder. Pour the mixture onto a piece of parchment paper and cover with a second sheet. Roll out as thin as possible. Transfer it, still in the parchment paper, to a sheet pan. Remove the top piece of parchment and place the pan in the oven. After a few minutes, the mixture will begin to bubble. After about 12 minutes, the bubbles covering the surface will have become smaller and the aroma of the cocoa nibs and hazelnuts will come through. Remove from the oven and set on a cooling rack.

Beetroot glass: Cut the beetroot into pieces and place, with all other ingredients, in a thermo blender. Heat to 80°C and blend on medium speed. If you do not have a thermo blender, you can blend the ingredients with a hand-held blender in a measuring cup set in a bain marie heated to exactly 80°C. Push the mixture through a fine strainer and let cool.

Take a template of your choice (for example, a flower shape or a round shape) Put the template on a silicone sheet and spread the beet mixture over it. Remove the template and dry in a 125°C oven for 35 minutes. Store in an airtight container with silicone granules.

Assembly: Cover the chocolate sponge with a thin layer of dark chocolate to create a protective shell then flip it over. Pour the cherry compote onto the sponge before it sets and leave to cool. Now pour the creamy dark chocolate onto the cherry compote and freeze.

Cut out the assembly a little smaller than the mold tc be used for the final cake. Pipe vanilla cream nto the molds, add the 'inserts' (i.e. the assembled sponge) with the sponge side up. Pour some more vanilla cream on the sides tc level with the sponge and freeze.

Coat the frozen cakes with the dark chocclate glaze. Pipe cream for topping with a star tip. Decorate with cherries, beetroot glass and cocoa nib crunchy.

GERMAN APPLE CAKE

Yield – A 23 cm round cake

Unsalted butter, soft – 125 gms
Caster sugar – 150 gms
Eggs – 2
All-purpose flour – 250 gms
Baking powder – ½ tsp
Milk – 125 ml
Apples – 4
Lemon juice – 20 ml

Topping
Ground cinnamon
Caster sugar

Grease a 23 cm spring form tin and line the base with baking paper.

Cream the butter and sugar. Add the eggs and beat well. Sift in half of the flour and beat to combine. Add the milk and remaining sifted flour alternately. Spread the mixture in the prepared tin.

Peel, quarter and thinly slice the apples. Put the slices in a bowl and drizzle the lemon juice over the slices to prevent discolouration.

Arrange the drained apples on top of the cake batter. Bake at 160°C in a preheated oven for 40 minutes or until risen and golden. While still warm, sprinkle with the caster sugar and cinnamon.

DESSERTS

Pour Some Sugar On Me!

VANILLA NUTMEG CUSTARD

Yield – 12 servings

Butter – 20 gms
Milk – 1 litre
Caster sugar – 250 gms
Seeds of ½ Vanilla bean
Eggs – 8
Cream, 35% – 250 gms
Almond powder – 50 gms
Nutmeg, grated – 5 gms

Grease the ramekins with butter. Heat the milk, sugar and vanilla seeds in a pan over a medium heat, stirring to dissolve the sugar. When it comes to a boil, reduce the heat slightly and simmer until the milk has reduced by half.

In a bowl, whisk the eggs until pale. Add the cream and whisk to combine, and then stir in the reduced milk, almond powder and nutmeg.

Pour the custard into the ramekins, then put these into a larger dish and pour in water to come halfway up the sides of the ramekins. Bake at 160°C in a preheated oven for 45 minutes or until the custard is just set. Remove from the oven and leave to cool for about 15 minutes before serving.

COFFEE CREME CARAMEL

Yield – 6 servings

Caster sugar – 160 gms
Milk – 280 ml
Cream, 35% – 105 gms
Instant coffee – 20 gms
Eggs – 3
Egg yolks – 2
Brown sugar – 50 gms

Put 100 gms of the sugar in a small heavy-bottomed saucepan and melt over medium heat until it turns a pale caramel colour. Immediately pour the hot caramel into the ramekins and swirl them around to coat the bottoms and sides. Leave to cool completely.

Combine the milk, cream, coffee and remaining sugar in a saucepan and gently bring to a boil over low heat, stirring to dissolve the sugar and coffee. In another bowl, whisk together the eggs and egg yolks for about two minutes until pale. Pour the boiling milk mixture into the egg mixture while whisking.

Divide the mixture into the ramekins and put them in the baking dish, then pour enough warm water into the dish to come halfway up the sides of the ramekins. Put the baking dish in the oven and bake at 105°C in a preheated oven for 45 minutes or until the tip of a sharp knife inserted into the middle of a ramekin comes out clean. Remove from the oven and transfer the pots to a wire rack to cool completely. Cover with plastic wrap, and then refrigerate at least four hours.

Sprinkle the tops of the pots with the brown sugar and caramelise with a blowtorch for a few seconds.

STRAWBERRY SUMAC & ROSE MESS

Yield – 4 servings

Rose water cream
Mascarpone – 160 gms
Greek yoghurt – 270 gms
Icing sugar, sifted – 15 gms
Rose water – 10 ml

Sumac syrup
Caster sugar – 40 gms
Pomegranate molasses – 2 tbsp
Sumac powder – 1 tsp

Strawberry sorbet
Water – 220 gms
Caster sugar – 160 gms
Atomized glucose – 120 gms
Sorbet stabilizer – 2.5 gms
Strawberry puree – 1160 gms

Swiss meringue kisses
Egg whites – 2
Caster sugar – 110 gms
Rose petals, dried

Topping
Strawberries, hulled, chopped – 200 gms
Meringues, broken roughly – 60 gms
Pomegranate seeds – 100 gms

Rose water cream: Place the mascarpone and yoghurt in a medium bowl and whisk until smooth. Add the icing sugar and rose water and continue to whisk, just until combined. Keep in the refrigerator until required.

Sumac syrup: Mix the caster sugar with 40 ml of boiling water and stir until the sugar dissolves. Add the pomegranate molasses and sumac, stir to combine and set aside.

Strawberry sorbet: Pre-mix half the sugar and stabilizer. Heat water. At 25°C add the glucose and rest of sugar. At 45°C, add the mix of sugar and stabilizer. Cook to 85°C. Cool quickly to 4°C. Add the strawberry puree and use hand blender to mix. Let it

mature for four hours in the refrigerator. Churn in an ice cream machine and freeze in quenelle shaped silicone molds.

Swiss meringue kisses: Place the egg whites and the caster sugar into the bowl of the stand mixer and mix to combine. Fill a saucepan with about 5 cm of water and bring to a simmer. Once the water is simmering, place the bowl with the egg white mixture over it to create a double boiler. Mix with the hand balloon whisk constantly for 3 minutes. The sugar should completely dissolve. Transfer the bowl onto the stand mixer and whisk on a high speed for 10 minutes or until the bowl is completely cool.

Place the meringue in a piping bag fitted with a round tip or star tip. On a flat baking tray lined with parchment paper, pipe 3.5 cm round dots of the meringue mixture. Sprinkle the kisses with dried rose petals and bake at 100°C in a preheated oven for 90 minutes. Then turn off the oven and leave the meringues in it for another 30-60 minutes to continue drying. Once done, the meringues should be crispy on the outside and chewy on the inside.

Topping: When ready to serve, divide the strawberries chopped lengthwise between four tall glasses, followed by the sumac syrup, broken pieces of meringue and rose water cream. Top with the pomegranate seeds and a quenelle of sorbet. Use up the remaining syrup and meringue. Serve immediately.

PANNA COTTA WITH PINE NUTS & HONEY

Yield – 4 servings

Cream, 35% – 300 gms
Milk – 100 gms
Caster sugar – 100 gms
Seeds of 1 Vanilla bean
Gelatin powder – 8 gms

Topping
Honey – 2 tbsp
Pine nuts, toasted – 40 gms

Panna Cotta is a chilled dessert popular throughout Italy.

Soften gelatin in 40 gms cold water and keep aside. In a saucepan, heat the cream, milk, sugar and vanilla seeds, taking the pan off the heat before it boils. Mix the gelatin into the hot cream-milk mixture. Divide the mixture among the four ramekins that have been brushed with oil. Place in the refrigerator overnight to set.

To turn out, dip the ramekins in boiling water, making sure you get no water in the bowls. This should slightly melt the edges, which will allow the panna cotta to slide out when the ramekins are inverted on to a plate.

Serve with a trickle of honey and some toasted pine nuts scattered on top.

CHOCOLATE PINEAPPLE VERRINE

Yield – 6 servings

Pineapple confit
Atomized glucose – 60 gms
Caster sugar – 60 gms
Pectin NH – 6 gms
Lemon juice – 4 gms
Pineapple puree – 375 gms
Gelatin powder – 1.5 gms

Chocolate mousse
Cream, 35% (A) – 100 gms
Milk – 100 gms
Egg yolks – 2
Caster sugar – 10 gms
Dark chocolate, 60-70%, melted – 270 gms
Cream, 35% (B), softly whipped – 450 gms

Brown sugar sponge
Brown sugar – 100 gms
Honey – 40 gms
All-purpose flour – 110 gms
Baking powder – 1 tsp
Eggs – 3
Unsalted butter, melted – 130 gms
Dark chocolate, 60-70%, grated – 60 gms
Coconut, dried, shredded – 20 gms

Coconut panna cotta
Coconut milk – 350 gms
Lemon grass, chopped – 40 gms
Cream, 35% – 150 gms
Caster sugar – 75 gms
Gelatin powder – 5 gms

Pineapple and lime mousseline
Egg whites – 3
Caster sugar – 135 gms
Water – 60 gms
Lime juice – 40 gms
Pineapple puree – 210 gms
Gelatin powder – 5 gms
Cream, 35%, slightly whipped – 150 gms

Compressed pineapple
Pineapple cubes – 100 gms
Sugar – 25 gms
Water – 25 gms
Bacardi rum – 20 gms

Coconut streusel
Unsalted butter, soft – 100 gms
Caster sugar – 100 gms
All-purpose flour – 100 gms
Coconut, dried, shredded – 70 gms
Fleur de sel – a pinch

Cocoa caviar
Water – 250 gms
Caster sugar – 50 gms
Agar agar – 2 gms
Cocoa powder – 30 gms
Sunflower oil – 1 litre

Pineapple confit Soften gelatin in 7.5 gms of cold water. Mix sugar and pectin. Heat puree in a saucepan. At 40°C, add glucose and mix with hand whisk. At 50°C, add sugar and pectin and keep whisking. Boil for one minute. Remove from heat; add lemon juice and gelatin. Cool to 40°C, mix with hand blender. Put a thin layer of confit in the verrine at the bottom.

Chocolate mousse: Boil cream (A) and milk. Pour on the egg yolks and sugar. Heat to 82°C and pour the Anglaise (heated egg yolks and sugar) onto the chocolate. Make an emulsion with hand blender. Cool to 35-40°C. Fold in cream (B). Pipe on top of confit and freeze.

Brown sugar sponge: Mix sugar, flour, baking powder and coconut in a bowl. Add honey, eggs and butter. Mix and add grated chocolate. Spread out as 1 cm high layer on a greased and parchment lined baking sheet. Bake at 165°C in a preheated oven. Cool and cut into rounds to fit top of verrine. Place on top of the mousse. Cut the rest of the cake into the size of semi-sphere molds for mousseline.

Coconut panna cotta: Soften gelatin in 25 gms cold water. Boil cream, lemon grass and sugar to a boil and infuse for 10 minutes. Strain and add coconut milk and gelatin. Cool the mix and add on top of sponge in the verrine.

Pineapple and lime mousseline: Soften gelatin in 25 gms cold water. Boil sugar and water to 121°C, pour over egg whites in the bowl of a stand mixer and whisk to make an Italian meringue. Warm some puree and add gelatin. Now mix rest of the puree and lime juice. Fold in the Italian meringue. Lastly, fold in the cream. Pour in semi-sphere molds. Cover with brown sugar sponge rounds and freeze. The semi-sphere mousseline goes on top of the coconut panna cotta, rounded side up.

Compressed pineapple: Make a syrup with sugar and water. Cool and add rum. Mix pineapple cubes with the syrup in a vacuum bag. Seal in the vacuum machine, once or twice. Refrigerate for two hours and then use the strained cubes and arrange on the sides of the mousseline.

Coconut streusel: Mix all the ingredients and combine till it all comes together in a ball. Cover with cling wrap and refrigerate. Then remove from refrigerator and grate roughly and spread on a parchment-lined tray. Bake at 160°C in a preheated oven till golden brown. Sprinkle streusel on top of pineapple and mousseline.

Cocoa caviar: Combine all the ingredients except the sunflower oil. Bring to a boil while continuously stirring to prevent the cocoa from sticking to the bottom of the saucepan. Leave to cool to 70°C. Separately, half fill a rectangular container (approximately 7 cm high) with the oil at 6°C. Fill a syringe with the cocoa base and drip the mix into the oil. Allow the caviar drops to gel and settle at the bottom of the container before pouring new drops. Take out the caviar drops and rinse in warm water.

Decorate with cocoa caviar and chocolate triangles.

MINT ICE CREAM

Yield – 10/12 servings

Milk – 500 ml
Cream, 35% – 500 gms
Egg yolks – 10
Caster sugar – 175 gms
Agar agar – 2.5 gms
Fresh mint leaves – 20 gms

Blanch the mint leaves in boiling water and then cool in ice-cold water and drain. Heat the milk and cream. Mix egg yolks and sugar with hand-held blender and pour in hot milk-cream to temper. Return to pan and cook to 75°C, stirring constantly. Add Agar agar with hand-held blender and heat to 81°C. Cool over an ice bath to 45°C. Puree one cup of mix with blanched mint in blender. Remix the mint ice cream mix with the original, incorporate well, and then strain through a fine mesh strainer. Churn in an ice cream machine and freeze. Serve scoops with sprigs of fresh mint.

EARL GREY & FIG MERINGUE

Yield – 8 servings

Meringues
Earl grey tea – 2 tsp
Caster sugar – 220 gms
Egg whites – 4
Corn flour – 10 gms
White vinegar – 1 tsp

Syrup-soaked figs
Earl grey tea – 1 tsp
Orange rind, long strips – 4
Caster sugar – 220 gms
Water – 125 ml
Orange juice, fresh – 60 ml
Figs, halved – 8

Sweetened yogurt
Greek yogurt – 500 gms
Vanilla extract – 1 tsp
Icing sugar – 10 gms

Topping
Pistachios
Mint sprigs

Meringues: Grind the tea with sugar. Beat egg whites in the bowl of a stand mixer with whisk attachment until soft peaks form. Gradually add tea-sugar mixture; beat until stiff and glossy. Sift corn flour over mixture, add vinegar; fold in with spatula. Pipe into circles with a large plain tip on a parchment lined tray. Bake meringues at 120°C in a preheated oven for 45 minutes or until firm to the touch. Cool in the turned-off oven with door ajar, for at least four hours or even overnight.

Syrup-soaked figs: Stir tea, rind, sugar, water and juice in a saucepan over medium heat until sugar dissolves. Bring to the boil; cook until syrup thickens slightly. Place halved figs in a large bowl and strain syrup over figs, gently stirring to combine the ingredients. Allow to cool.

Sweetened yogurt: Beat ingredients in a medium bowl until soft peaks form.

Topping: Just before serving, spread sweetened yogurt on the meringue. Top with drained figs and then pour some syrup over figs. Sprinkle with pistachios and decorate with sprigs of mint.

SALTED CARAMEL ICE CREAM

Yield – 6/8 servings

Candied walnuts
Liquid glucose– 170 gms
Maple syrup – 160 gms
Vanilla extract – 1 tsp
Fleur de sel – a pinch
Walnuts, roasted,
chopped – 90 gms

Salted caramel ice cream
Milk – 550 gms
Caster sugar (A) – 75 gms
Atomized glucose – 45 gms
Egg yolk – 1
Cream, 35% – 30 gms
Unsalted butter – 20 gms
Milk powder – 30 gms
Caster sugar (B) – 85 gms
Ice cream stabilizer – 5 gms
Fleur de sel – 2 gms

Candied walnuts: Bring glucose, maple syrup, vanilla extract, and salt to a boil in a saucepan
Stir in walnuts and cook for about three minutes until walnuts are warmed through. Cool and transfer to a glass jar with a lid. This can be stored in the refrigerator for up to a month.

Salted caramel ice cream: Make a dark caramel with sugar (B). Cool it with cream and butter. Add the milk. At 20°C, add the milk powder and atomized glucose. At 30°C, add the egg yolk and salt. At 45°C, add the sugar (A) previously combined with the stabilizer. Pasteurize the mixture to 85°C and stir. Cool down quickly to 4°C and leave to mature for at least four hours in a refrigerator. Churn in an ice cream machine and freeze. Serve with candied walnuts.

PLUM & YOGURT MEDLEY

Yield – 4 servings

Yogurt pudding
Gelatin powder – 7 gms
Cream, 35% – 200 gms
Milk – 200 gms
Caster sugar – 100 gms
Seeds of ½ Vanilla bean
Zest of ½ orange, grated
Greek yogurt – 200 gms

Poached plums
Water – 250 ml
Pernod (Anise flavoured spirit) – 125 ml
Plums, quartered – 4
Caster sugar – 100 gms
Seeds of ½ Vanilla bean
Lemon juice – 4 tbsp
Pistachio, slivered – 20 gms

Hazelnut streusel
All-purpose flour – 50 gms
Brown sugar – 60 gms
Cinnamon, ground – 1 tsp
Unsalted butter – 50 gms
Hazelnuts, toasted, chopped – 75 gms

Whipped chocolate ganache
Dark chocolate, 60-70% – 180 gms
Cream, 35% – 150 gms

Basil ice cream
Basil leaves – 50 gms
Milk – 500 ml
Cream, 35% – 250 gms
Caster sugar – 150 gms
Zest of 1 lemon
Fleur de sel – a pinch
Egg yolks – 6

Yogurt pudding: Soften the gelatin in 35 gms cold water and keep aside. Pour the cream and milk into a small saucepan and add sugar, vanilla seeds and orange zest. Place over medium heat, bring to a simmer and then remove immediately. Add the gelatin. Put yogurt in a medium mixing bowl and whisk constantly while pouring in the hot milk and cream in a slow stream. Pour the mixture into four ramekins and leave to set in the refrigerator for at least five hours.

Poached plums: Put the water, Pernod, vanilla seeds and sugar in a medium saucepan. Bring to a boil and add the quartered plums. Simmer gently for 8 to 12 minutes depending on the ripeness of the plums; they need to be completely soft. Remove from the heat and leave to cool in the pan. Once cool, stir in the lemon juice and refrigerate.

Hazelnut streusel: In a food processor, combine the flour, brown sugar, cinnamon and butter and process until crumbly. Transfer to a bowl and stir in the chopped hazelnuts. Spread on a parchment lined tray and bake at 160°C in a preheated oven for 10-15 minutes until golden brown.

Whipped chocolate ganache: In a small saucepan, boil the cream and then remove from heat. Pour hot cream over chocolate and allow to rest for five minutes. Mix ganache until smooth. Chill for approximately two hours. Remove from refrigerator and pour into the bowl of a stand mixer with whisk attachment. Beat on low speed for 30-40 seconds until colour turns to a lighter brown. At this point the ganache should hold its shape. Place in piping bag.

Basil ice cream: Combine basil, milk, cream, sugar, zest, salt, and yolks in a blender and puree until smooth. Pour into a saucepan and heat gently until sugar dissolves. Remove from heat and pour through a fine strainer and then chill in the refrigerator. Churn in an ice cream maker and then freeze.

Assembly: Arrange streusel on plates. Pipe whipped chocolate ganache with plain tip. Remove the yogurt pudding from the mold and overturn onto serving plates. Arrange the plums and generously pour the syrup over and around the pudding. Sprinkle with pistachios. Alongside put 2-3 scoops of basil ice cream. Garnish with mint leaves.

DAIRY WHITE

Yield – 4/6 servings

Yogurt sorbet
Caster sugar – 80 gms
Pectin NH – 5 gms
Milk – 200 ml
Invert sugar – 65 gms
Lemon juice – 20 ml
Greek yogurt – 480 gms

Milk meringue
Milk – 250 ml
Egg white – 2
Egg white powder – 15 gms
Caster sugar – 100 gms
Xantana – 6 gms
Versawhip – 1.5 gms

Coconut milk sago
Tapioca pearls – 150 gms
Coconut cream – 150 gms
Caster sugar – 25 gms
Water – 25 gms

Coconut snow
Maltodextrin – 40 gms
Coconut oil – 60 gms
Icing sugar – 15 gms

Yogurt sorbet: Heat milk and invert sugar to 50°C. Mix the pectin and sugar in a small bowl and add to milk and boil. Cool slightly and add yogurt & lemon juice and mix using a hand blender. Churn in an ice cream machine and freeze in silicone molds, using different shapes.

Milk meringue: Place all the ingredients in the bowl of a stand mixer and mix on a low speed for two minutes and then on high for six minutes. Spread out on dehydrator mats to a 3 cm thickness and dehydrate overnight.

Coconut milk sago: Boil sugar and water in a pan and keep aside. Cook the tapioca in the boiling water until tender. Remove and cool under cold running water. Mix the coconut cream and sugar syrup together and slowly add to the sago until it forms a smooth but firm mix. Add sugar syrup to adjust the consistency if required.

Coconut snow: Mix Maltodextrin, coconut oil and icing sugar in a food processor. Beat while scraping down the sides of bowl occasionally with a spatula until crumbs form.

Assembly: Arrange the sorbet, milk meringue, milk sago and coconut snow on a platter. Decorate as desired.

Milk meringue and coconut snow can also be used to decorate other plated desserts.

CHOCOLATE CARAMEL TOWERS

Yield – 6 servings

Caramel
Cream, 35% – 60 gms
Unsalted butter – 60 gms
Brown sugar – 75 gms
Liquid glucose – 15 gms
Vanilla extract – ½ tsp

Panna cotta
Gelatin powder – 5 gms
Cream, 35% – 240 gms
Caster sugar – 50 gms
Dark chocolate, 60-70%, melted – 175 gms
Sour cream – 80 gms

Topping
Cream, 35% – 100 gms
Icing sugar – 15 gms
Cocoa powder
Chocolate squares

Caramel: In a medium heavy saucepan, stir together cream butter, brown sugar, and glucose. Bring to a boil over medium-high heat, whisking occasionally; reduce heat to medium. Boil gently for two additional minutes. Remove from heat; stir in vanilla.

Panna cotta: Soften gelatin in 25 gms cold water and keep aside. In a medium saucepan, combine cream and the sugar. Heat over medium-low heat until the mixture almost comes to a boil. Remove from heat. Add gelatin; stir until it dissolves. Pour over chocolate and let it stand for five minutes. Stir to mix in chocolate. Whisk in sour cream.

Assembly: Fill in half of tall glasses with the chocolate panna cotta. Chill for 20 minutes or until just set. Divide caramel evenly among the glasses; chill for 15 minutes. Pour in the remaining chocolate mixture. Chill for another 30 minutes. Whisk cream and icing sugar until soft peaks form. To serve, top the panna cotta with a dollop of whipped cream-sugar and a chocolate square if desired. Sprinkle lightly with cocoa powder.

PINEAPPLE CARPACCIO

Yield – A 25 cm serving platter

Vanilla salt
Fleur de sel – 125 gms
Seeds of 1 Vanilla bean

Pineapple Carpaccio
Pineapple, ripened – 1
Pomegranate – 1
Mint leaves – small bunch

Vanilla salt: Put the salt and vanilla seeds into a bowl and mix well. Place in an airtight container and use as required in baking or savoury dishes. The mixture will keep indefinitely.

Pineapple carpaccio: Cut off the ends of the pineapple then slice off the entire skin, keeping the fruit whole. Cut the pineapple width ways into many slices about 1 mm thick. Set aside.

Cut the pomegranate in half horizontally. Hold each half in turn over a bowl and smack the skin with the back of a wooden spoon so that the seeds drop into the bowl. Reserve any juice that comes out while removing the seeds.

To serve, sprinkle a serving platter with a little vanilla salt. Arrange the pineapple slices over it and then sprinkle again with a little more vanilla salt. Now sprinkle the pomegranate seeds and juice over the sliced pineapples. Finish with a few shredded mint leaves.

MOCHA BERRY VERRINE

Yield – 24 servings

Blackberry jelly
Caster sugar – 50 gms
Locust bean gum – 3 gms
Water, purified – 35 gms
Blackberry puree – 250 gms
Raspberry puree – 105 gms
Gelatin powder – 10 gms

Cocoa crumble
Unsalted butter, soft – 100 gms
All-purpose flour – 120 gms
Almond powder – 50 gms
Sugar – 100 gms
Cocoa powder – 20 gms
Baking soda – a pinch
Fleur de sel – ¼ tsp

Coffee mousse
Milk – 60 ml
Gelatin powder – 4 gms
Milk chocolate, melted – 150 gms
Espresso coffee – 70 ml
Egg white powder – 7.5 gms
Dextrose – 45 gms
Cream, 35%, softly whipped – 175 gms

Blackberry cremeux
Cream, 35% – 210 gms
Caster sugar – 45 gms
Eggs yolks – 3
Blackberry puree – 140 gms
Gelatin powder – 4 gms

Blackberry dry meringue
Blackberry puree – 125 gms
Versawhip – 2.5 gms
Caster sugar – 75 gms

Caramelised white chocolate
White chocolate – 300 gms

Chocolate vermicelli
Gelatin powder – 4 gms
Milk – 150 ml
Liquid glucose – 7.5 gms
Caramelised white chocolate – 275 gms
(recipe on next page)
Cream, 35%, cold – 250 gms

Blackberry jelly: Soften gelatin in 50 gms cold water and set aside. Mix sugar and carob gum together. Add blackberry & raspberry puree to water and bring to a boil and remove from heat. Add gelatin and mix. Pour a little into each of the verrines and then pour the rest in flower shaped silicone molds for decoration.

Cocoa crumble: Mix all the ingredients in a food processor and homogenize. Make into a log, wrap in cling film and refrigerate overnight. Grate roughly on a parchment lined tray and bake at 160°C in a preheated oven for 15 minutes till cooked. Cool and sprinkle some on top of jelly in each verrine.

Coffee mousse: Soften gelatin in 20 gms cold water. Mix the coffee, egg white powder and dextrose with a hand blender. Leave to stand for 10 minutes, and whisk again to make a coffee meringue. Heat the milk to 60°C. Add gelatin and mix. Pour over melted chocolate and emulsify with a hand blender. When the base is 34°C, gently fold whipped cream. Fold in the coffee meringue. Pour over the crumble in the verrines and freeze.

Blackberry cremeux: Soften gelatin in 20 gms cold water and keep aside. In a saucepan, bring the cream and sugar to a boil and then add in the egg yolks. Cook the custard to 84°C. Add the gelatin. Once it has dissolved, cool the mixture down to 30°C and mix in the blackberry puree. Pour into a piping bag. Put a thin layer on top of coffee mousse and freeze again.

Blackberry dry meringue: Mix the puree with the Versawhip in a bowl of stand mixer and whisk. Add the sugar in three batches during the whipping process, until obtaining a firm meringue. Put in piping bag with a plain tip. Pipe small rounds on parchment lined baking sheet. Dehydrate for a minimum of 6 hours at 40°C until dry and crunchy.

Caramelised white chocolate: Place the chocolate on a sheet pan lined with a silicone baking mat and place in preheated oven at 100°C for 10 minutes. Remove the pan from the oven and stir the chocolate on the sheet pan. Continue doing this in 10-minute intervals until colour turns a deep golden brown. During the cooking process, the chocolate may look lumpy and unpleasant, keep stirring, as it will smoothen out and caramelise. If the chocolate remains lumpy, smoothen it with an immersion blender.

Chocolate vermicelli: Soften gelatin in 20 gms cold water and keep aside. In a saucepan, heat milk and glucose syrup over medium heat until glucose is dissolved. Pour over the chocolate using an immersion blender to combine the mixture. Add the cold cream, blending while pouring in and then strain. Cover the top with cling wrap. Chill overnight in the refrigerator before using. Pipe with a vermicelli-piping tip on top of blackberry cremeux in the verrines.

Decorate with blackberry meringues and jelly flowers.

SEVEN SHADES OF BROWN

Yield – 6/8 servings

Vanilla ice cream
Milk – 575 gms
Caster sugar – 145 gms
Atomized glucose – 60 gms
Seeds of 2 Vanilla beans
Egg yolks – 2
Cream, 35% – 225 gms
Milk powder – 40 gms
Ice cream stabilizer – 3 gms

Dark chocolate ice cream
Water – 510 gms
Milk powder – 90 gms
Cream, 35% – 100 gms
Egg yolk – 1
Dextrose – 45 gms
Fructose – 20 gms
Caster sugar – 100 gms
Cocoa powder – 10 gms
Dark chocolate, 60-70% – 105 gms
Ice cream stabilizer – 5 gms

Coffee ice cream
Coffee beans, dark roasted, ground – 30 gms
Milk – 300 ml
Brown sugar – 100 gms
Egg yolks – 3
Cream, 35% – 240 gms

Chocolate sauce
Whole milk – 250 ml
Cocoa powder – 15 gms
Caster sugar – 50 gms
Egg yolks – 2

Chocolate fudge
Seed of 1 Vanilla bean
Cream, 35% – 250 gms
Caster sugar – 200 gms
Honey – 30 gms
Dark chocolate, 60-70% – 100 gms
Unsalted butter – 40 gms

Wafer cups
Eggs – 2
Fleur de sel – ¼ tsp
Caster sugar – 130 gms
Grapeseed oil – 30 gms
All-purpose flour – 140 gms
Vanilla extract – 1 tsp

Vanilla ice cream: Heat up the milk and the cream. At 20°C, add half of the caster sugar, milk powder and the glucose then add the vanilla seeds. At 30°C add the egg yolks and at 45°C, the stabilizer mixed with the rest of the sugar. Cook to 85°C and strain. Quickly cool down to 4°C and leave to mature for at least four hours. Mix again with hand blender and churn in an ice cream machine. Freeze.

Dark chocolate ice cream: Mix stabilizer with sugar and cocoa powder. Mix water and milk powder in a pan and heat. At 30°C add the sugars and at 45°C, add the stabilizer mix and heat to 85°C. Remove from heat and pour over chocolate, mix and cool. Once it is cold, add the cream and egg yolk. Leave to mature for at least 10 hours in refrigerator. Churn in the ice cream machine and freeze.

Coffee ice cream: Heat the milk in a pan to nearly boiling point and pour over the coffee. Leave to stand for four minutes. Meanwhile, in a large bowl, beat the sugar and egg yolks until light. Pour the milk over, whisking all the time. Strain the mixture back into the pan through a fine sieve. Cook the custard over a low heat for 1-2 minutes, stirring till it reaches 85°C. Cool and add cream and keep in refrigerator to mature for at least four hours. Mix again and churn in an ice cream machine and then freeze.

Chocolate sauce: Whisk the milk and cocoa powder together, beating constantly. Whisk the sugar and egg yolks together in a bowl, then pour over the milk and cocoa mixture, stir well and pour into a pan. Cook over a moderate heat, stirring slowly and continuously, until the mixture reaches 85°C. Strain the mixture through a fine-mesh strainer and leave to cool completely.

Chocolate fudge: Mix the cream, sugar, honey, vanilla bean, chocolate, and butter in a pan. Bring the mixture to a boiling point and cook over a medium heat, stirring frequently. Cook to 110°C and pour the boiling mixture into a heatproof bowl and allow it to cool, stirring constantly. When the fudge thickens, pour it into a mold and leave to harden then cut into small pieces.

Wafer cups: Preheat the WaffleCone machine. Stir the eggs and salt in a small bowl with a fork until well blended. Beat in, for about one minute, the sugar and blend until sugar is incorporated and the eggs have lightened in colour. Stir in the oil. Add the flour and stir slowly until all flour is moistened. Beat another 15 seconds to incorporate the flour and remove all lumps. Stir in the vanilla extract. Spoon three tablespoons of batter in the centre or slightly above centre of the iron. Close the lid, lock the latch, and bake for one minute and then check if it's a golden colour. Cook an additional 20 to 40 seconds if necessary. Quickly remove the waffle onto a clean cloth towel. Press and put in an inverted muffin mold to make a cup shape. Let it cool. Serve scoops of chocolate, vanilla and coffee ice cream in the wafer cups. Garnish with pieces of fudge and chocolate sauce.

TROPICAL BONANZA

Yield – 10/12 servings

Passion fruit air bubbles
Passion fruit puree – 150 gms
Gelatin powder – 6 gms
Caster sugar – 15 gms

Coconut streusel
Almond powder – 50 gms
Icing sugar – 50 gms
Flour – 25 gms
Coconut, shredded,
dried – 25 gms
Unsalted butter – 50 gms
Fleur de sel – a pinch

Chocolate crisp
White chocolate – 40 gms
Cocoa butter – 15 gms
Brown sugar – 25 gms
Chopped almonds – 25 gms
Paillete feuilletine – 25 gms
Coconut streusel – 50 gms
(recipe on next page)

Coconut espuma
Coconut puree – 400 gms
Gelatin powder – 2 gms
Water – 50 gms
Sugar – 30 gms

Guava sorbet
Water (A) – 220 ml
Caster sugar – 160 gms
Atomised glucose – 115 gms
Sorbet stabiliser – 2.5 gms
Guava puree – 250 gms
Water (B) – 360 ml

Raspberry coulis
Raspberries – 250 gms
Icing sugar – 15 gms
Lemon juice – 2 tsp
Xantana – 2 gms

Passion fruit air bubbles: Soften the gelatin in 30 gms cold water and keep aside. Mix sugar and 15 ml water and give one boil to make a syrup. Place the passion fruit juice and sugar syrup in a bowl and heat a little. Add gelatin and dissolve. Gently beat with a whisk to obtain a frothy mixture. Fill in truffle silicone molds and freeze.

Coconut streusel: Mix all the ingredients in a food processor. Crumble and place on a parchment lined tray. Keep in refrigerator overnight. Then bake crumble at 160°C in a preheated oven for 10 minutes. Place the still-soft streusel in small balls on a sheet. Place briefly in a cool place to allow the mixture to become firm. Then leave to dry in a plastic box and store at room temperature.

Chocolate crisp: Melt the chocolate and cocoa butter, add all the other ingredients and mix well and keep ready.

Coconut espuma: Soften gelatin in 10 gms of cold water. Heat water and sugar and add the gelatin to dissolve. Add coconut puree and place the preparation in a siphon. Insert one N2O cartridge, leave to rest in a cool place for one hour.

Guava sorbet: Mix half of the sugar with stabiliser. Heat water (A) to 25°C and add remaining sugar and glucose. At 45°C, add the stabiliser mixed with sugar. Heat to 85°C. Cool rapidly to 4°C. Add guava puree and water (B) and mix with hand blender. Refrigerate overnight. Churn in ice-cream machine, freeze in decorative silicone molds.

Raspberry coulis: Heat all the ingredients until the raspberries start to break down. Blend in a food processor and strain. Mix Xantana and freeze in small silicone molds.

Assembly: Put all the ingredients in layers in each verrine in a decorative fashion. Top with coconut espuma.

BANANA ROULETTE

Yield – 8 servings

Banana ice cream
Caster sugar – 160 gms
Honey – 5 gms
Milk – 100 ml
Cream – 300 ml
Banana, peeled – 140 gms

Banana paper
Banana, peeled – 100 gms
Caster sugar – 30 gms
All-purpose flour – 10 gms
Unsalted butter, melted – 30 gms
Milk – 25 ml

Chocolate crumble
All-purpose flour – 125 gms
Cocoa powder – 25 gms
Unsalted butter, cold – 75 gms
Muscovado sugar – 75 gms
Fleur de sel – 2 gms

Salted caramel sauce
Cream, 35% (A) – 100 gms
Caster sugar – 100 gms
Liquid Glucose – 50 gms
Cream, 35% (B) – 50 gms
Unsalted butter, soft – 25 gms
Fleur de sel – 2 gms

Banana ice cream: Dissolve the sugar and honey in the milk and add the cream. Add the banana in pieces. Freeze the mixture. Remove from freezer and churn the mixture in an ice cream machine. Re-freeze and then take out and re-churn again one more time. Now freeze in silicone molds.

Banana paper: Mash the banana and mix with all the other ingredients in a blender until you have a homogeneous mixture. Spread out onto silicone mats as thinly and evenly as possible. Place in the freezer. Once hardened, bake at 160°C in a preheated oven for about 10 minutes until crunchy and golden brown. Break into pieces and store in an airtight container.

Chocolate crumble: Mix the flour, cocoa, sugar and salt together in a medium bowl and then rub the butter in with fingers. Add a few drops of cold water to the mixture to bring it together, leaving some chunks in among the rubber-like crumbs. Spread on a silicone mat and refrigerate for two hours. Bake at 160°C in a preheated oven for 8-10 minutes.

Salted caramel sauce: Place cream (A), sugar and glucose in a large, heavy-based saucepan. Place the saucepan over medium heat and stir constantly with a hand whisk. Cook the mixture until it reaches 118°C. Remove from the heat. Stir in the remaining cream (B), butter and salt. Leave to cool naturally in the pan before pouring into a jar and storing in a cool, dark place. Arrange all the elements decoratively on a platter.

PALET D'OR WITH NUTELLA ICE CREAM

Yield – 6 servings

Nutella ice cream
Milk – 550 gms
Liquid glucose – 35 gms
Egg yolks – 8
Caster sugar – 25 gms
Nutella – 200 gms

Gin gelee
Gelatin powder – 8 gms
Gin – 250 ml

Cake
Unsalted butter – 130 gms
Icing sugar – 110 gms
Eggs, separated – 6
Dark chocolate, 60-70%, melted – 130 gms
Caster sugar – 200 gms
All-purpose flour – 130 gms

Chocolate tuiles
Egg whites – 2
Caster sugar – 90 gms
All-purpose flour – 55 gms
Cocoa powder – 1 tsp
Unsalted butter, melted – 55 gms

Passion fruit cream
Cream, 35% – 125 gms
Caster sugar – 50 gms
Passion fruit juice – 40 ml

Chocolate ganache
Cream, 35% – 150 gms
Dark chocolate, 60-70% – 175 gms
Liquid glucose – 30 gms
Unsalted butter – 30 gms

Topping
Finely crushed cocoa nibs
Bronze powder

Nutella ice cream: Put the milk and liquid glucose into a saucepan and stir over low heat until the glucose has melted. Slowly bring to a boil. Meanwhile, beat the egg yolks and sugar in a bowl, and then stir in the Nutella; the mixture will be quite thick. As soon as the milk starts to boil, take off the heat and slowly pour onto the egg mixture until smooth. Pass through a fine sieve into a clean pan. Stir over a low heat until the custard thickens enough to lightly coat the back of the spoon. Strain the custard through a fine sieve into a bowl. Cool, churn in an ice cream machine and freeze in quenelle shaped silicone molds.

Gin gelee: Soften the gelatin in 40 gms cold water. Warm the gin in a small pan but don't let it boil; take off the heat. Add gelatin to the gin, stirring until dissolved. Pour into a shallow container and cool completely. Cover and chill overnight to set the jelly.

Cake: Beat the butter and icing sugar together in a large bowl until pale and creamy. Gradually beat in the egg yolks, and then fold in the melted chocolate. Whisk the egg whites in a clean, dry bowl to firm peaks using an electric beater. Slowly whisk in the caster sugar, a tablespoonful at a time, to make a firm meringue. Carefully fold the flour into the chocolate batter, and then fold in the meringue. Spread the mixture in a 23 x 23 cm square tin, lined with parchment. Bake at 160°C in a preheated oven for 50 minutes to one hour until the cake feels springy when lightly pressed and a skewer inserted into the centre comes out clean. Leave to cool in the tin.

Chocolate tuiles: Put the egg whites and sugar in a bowl and lightly beat with a fork. Sift in the flour with the cocoa powder and stir to mix well. Add the butter and stir until evenly blended. Using a palette knife spread a few thin strips of the tuile mixture on parchment lined baking sheet. Bake tuiles at 160°C in a preheated oven for 7-8 minutes until brown at the edges and shows a matt appearance. Leave to cool for a minute or two. Just before they set, while still pliable, lift each tuile with a palette knife and twist on a rod. Leave to cool and set; they will become crisp and brittle. Store in an airtight container until ready to serve.

Passion fruit cream: Put the cream and sugar in a small saucepan and stir over a low heat until the sugar has dissolved. Increase the heat and let bubble for three minutes. Lower the heat, stir in the passion fruit juice and let it simmer for a further two minutes or until thickened to a pouring cream consistency. Leave to cool.

Chocolate ganache: Put all the ingredients for the ganache into a double boiler. Stir until the mixture is smooth and shiny. Keep warm while assembling the dessert.

Assembly: Trim the sides and top of the cake to even out, then cut into 12 or 16 neat squares. Spread a layer of ganache over one square then sandwich with another, with the flat side facing upwards. Repeat with the remaining cake squares. Place the cake sandwiches on a wire rack set over a baking tray. Pipe three rosettes of ganache on top. Sprinkle with bronze coated cocoa nibs. Use chocolate decoration on one side.

To plate, spoon the passion fruit cream decoratively onto the serving plates. Using a clean palette knife, carefully lift a piece the cake onto each plate. Put a spoonful of gin gelee alongside. Serve with Nutella ice cream quenelles and tuiles.

PALET D'OR WITH NUTELLA ICE CREAM

SAFFRON & ORANGE SORBET

Yield – 12 servings

Dehydrated milk foam
Milk – 500 ml
Liquid glucose – 100 gms

Sorbet
Water – 180 gms
Sugar – 45 gms
Dextrose – 20 gms
Sorbet stabilizer – 4 gms
Cointreau – 20 gms
Candied orange zest, pureed – 60 gms
Orange juice – 650 gms
Honey – 10 gms
Saffron – 1 gm

Topping
Balsamic syrup
Mint sprigs

Dehydrated milk foam: Line a 20 x 30 cm rimmed baking sheet with acetate. In a medium saucepan, heat the milk and glucose until just under a boil. Remove from the heat and froth with a hand blender. Scoop the foam out with a large spoon onto the prepared baking sheet. Dry this in the oven overnight at 80°C for 8 to 9 hours. Allow the foam to cool before breaking it into pieces. Store the dehydrated foam in an airtight container.

Sorbet: Mix the water, sugars and stabilizer and heat to 85°C. Meanwhile, combine the orange juice, liqueur, orange zest, saffron and honey. Pour the sugar-stabilizer mixture over the other mix. Beat with the hand blender and then leave in a refrigerator overnight to mature. Churn in an ice cream machine and set the sorbet in a cube silicone mold and freeze.

Decorate with dehydrated milk foam and balsamic syrup. Serve cold.

COFFEE TEA WHIP

Yield – 4 servings

Tea whip
Cream, 35% – 160 gms
Cinnamon, ground – ½ tsp
Cardamom, ground – ¼ tsp
Ginger, ground – ¼ tsp
Cloves, ground – a pinch
Black tea, powder – ¼ tsp
Icing sugar – 30 gms

Espresso granita
Hot espresso – 750 ml
Caster sugar – 50 gms

Using decaf-coffee for the espresso can reduce the level of caffeine.

Tea whip: Whisk the cream to soft peaks. Beat in the spices and sugar. Cover and store in the refrigerator for at least 30 minutes.

Espresso granita: Combine the hot espresso and sugar. Whisk very well to dissolve the sugar. Pour into a rectangular pan, and place in the freezer. Scrape the espresso mix every 30 minutes for 2-3 hours with a fork to 'fluff' up the ice crystals. Serve the granita with scoops of the tea whipped cream on top. Decorate as desired.

COCONUT TAMARIND ICE CREAM

Yield – 8/10 servings

Black rice
Black rice – 250 gms
Coconut milk – 150 ml
Caster sugar – 60 gms

Coconut tamarind ice cream
Coconut cream – 200 gms
Cream, 35% – 500 gms
Seeds of 1 Vanilla bean
Egg yolks – 8
Caster sugar – 150 gms
Tamarind paste – 2 tbsp

Topping
Coconut, fresh, shredded – 40 gms
Palm sugar – 45 gms
Fleur de sel – a pinch
Coconut milk – 100 gms

Black rice: Soak the black rice in warm water overnight. Drain; place the rice in a steamer and steam for 20 minutes on high heat. Combine half the coconut milk with the sugar and mix thoroughly into the hot steamed rice. Set aside.

Coconut tamarind ice cream: Mix the coconut cream, milk and vanilla seeds in a saucepan and bring to boiling point. Meanwhile, whisk the egg yolks and sugar. Slowly add half the hot coconut-vanilla-milk mixture to the egg yolk mixture, stirring all the time. Now stir this mixture into the remaining half hot milk mixture and cook over low heat, stirring constantly until 83°C. Strain immediately into a bowl set over an iced water bath. Stir to bring down the temperature and then mix in the tamarind paste. Transfer to the refrigerator and leave to chill overnight. Churn in an ice cream machine and freeze.

Topping: Place the shredded coconut, coconut milk, palm sugar and salt in a medium saucepan and cook on high heat to reduce until almost dry. Use as topping for the black rice. Serve ice cream scoops over black rice and coconut. Sprinkle with a few chia seeds on top.

BASBOUSA

Yield – 8/10 servings

Cake
Vegetable oil – 180 ml
Cream, 35% – 350 ml
Coconut, dried, shredded – 100 gms
All-purpose flour – 160 gms
Semolina – 250 gms
Pistachio nuts, ground – 50 gms
Baking powder – 4 tsp
Eggs – 6
Caster sugar – 300 gms

Lemon curd
Zest of 2 lemons
Caster sugar – 200 gms
Eggs – 3
Egg yolks – 3
Lemon juice – 70 gms
Unsalted butter – 110 gms

Syrup
Water – 375 ml
Sugar – 330 gms
Cinnamon, ground – 1 tsp

Chantilly
Cream, 35%, cold – 250 gms
Caster sugar – 25 gms
Vanilla extract – ½ tsp

Topping
Cherry preserves

Cake: Mix the vegetable oil and cream in a large bowl. Combine the coconut, flour, semolina, ground pistachios, and baking powder in a separate bowl. Stir into the oil mixture. Beat the eggs and sugar in the bowl of a stand mixer fitted with the whisk attachment on high speed for eight minutes until pale and fluffy. Gently fold the beaten eggs into the semolina mix. Pour the batter into greased and parchment lined 30 x 30 cm baking pan. Bake at 180°C in a preheated oven for 35 minutes, or until the cake turns golden and a skewer inserted into the centre comes out clean.

Syrup: Bring the water, sugar, and cinnamon to a boil in a small saucepan. Lower the heat and simmer for 15 minutes. Cool slightly. Take the cake out of the oven and pour the syrup evenly over the warm cake. Cool completely and store in an airtight container.

Lemon curd: Blend the sugar and the lemon zest in a food processor. Mix with eggs and egg yolks, and cook to a slight boil. Remove from heat, add butter and emulsify with a hand blender. Store in the refrigerator and allow to crystallize overnight.

Chantilly: Place the cold cream in the bowl of a stand mixer with the whisk attachment that has been previously cooled in the freezer. Start to whip while sprinkling in the sugar with the vanilla. Once ready, store in the refrigerator. Cut the cake into small squares and top each square with a dollop of cherry preserves. Serve with lemon curd and Chantilly.

PRALINE & LEMON MELANGE

Yield – 15/20 servings

Praline
Almonds, with skin – 330 gms
Hazelnuts – 330 gms
Water – 85 gms
Caster sugar – 330 gms

Candied lemons
Lemons – 3
Caster sugar (A) – as required
Caster sugar (B) – 250 gms

Chocolate crunch
Milk chocolate – 35 gms
Praline – 35 gms
(recipe below)
Feuilletine – 35 gms

Praline Ice cream
Milk – 580 gms
Milk powder – 2 gms
Invert sugar – 55 gms
Cream, 35% – 25 gms
Seeds of 1 Vanilla bean
Praline – 170 gms
(recipe below)
Caster sugar (A) – 60 gms
Ice cream stabilizer – 3 gms
Egg yolks – 3
Caster sugar (B) – 55 gms

Praline: Roast the nuts in a baking sheet at 160°C in a preheated oven for 20-30 minutes and then cool. Heat sugar and water in a heavy saucepan. Cook to approximately 180°C till a nice caramel colour forms. Pour in a baking sheet and let it cool. Crush the caramel into pieces. Mix in the roasted nuts and grind in a heavy-duty mixer to a fine paste. While grinding the temperature of the praline should not go over 40°C. If it is getting too hot, wait for a while for it to cool and then grind again.

Candied lemons: Cut the lemons into slices. Put in boiling water and drain. Repeat once again. Weigh the lemons and take the same weight of sugar (A). Put the lemon slices in a saucepan. Add half the sugar (A). Cover with water. Let the lemons simmer over low heat for 20 minutes and then cool. Add the remaining sugar (B), cover with water and again simmer on low heat for 20 minutes. Cool and cut into small cubes.

Chocolate crunch: Melt the milk chocolate at about 40°C. Mix the praline and the chocolate. Carefully add the feuilletine. Spread the chocolate feuilletine between two parchment sheets to about 2 mm thick. Leave to crystallise. Break the crunch into small pieces. Set aside.

Praline ice cream: Heat the milk, milk powder, invert sugar, cream and vanilla seeds between 25°C and 40°C. Add the praline. Mix the caster sugar (A) and the ice cream stabilizer by pouring into the pan while whisking. Add the egg yolks and caster sugar (B), previously whisked until pale. Cook at 83°C. Emulsify mixture with hand blender. Cool quickly and then leave to mature for 24 hours. Churn in an ice cream machine, remove and then mix in 100 gms of candied lemon. Freeze in any shaped silicone mold. Serve with chocolate crunch and candied lemon on top.

MANGO & CARDAMOM ICE CREAM

Yield – 10/12 servings

Ice cream
Mangoes, peeled, chopped – 650 gms
Greek yogurt – 225 gms
Cream, 35% – 150 gms
Green cardamom, ground – 1 tsp
Rose water – 2 tsp
Honey – 120 gms
Lemon juice – 1½ tbsp

Biscuits
Egg white – 1
Icing sugar – 50 gms
Brazil nuts, finely sliced – 130 gms
Zest of 1 orange, grated

Ice cream: Put all the ingredients in a blender and blitz for a minute until smooth. Churn in an ice cream machine and freeze.

Biscuits: Put the egg white and icing sugar in a medium bowl and whisk until smooth. Add the nuts and orange zest and stir to combine. Spoon 4 cm-wide dollops of the biscuit mix on the parchment lined tray, spacing them well apart. Dip the spoon in water, to prevent it sticking, and then gently flatten each dollop into a 6 cm round using the back of the spoon. Bake at 150°C in a preheated oven for 15 minutes, until starting to turn golden-brown, then remove from the oven and set aside to cool. Serve alongside the ice cream.

MANGO JELLY WITH TAPIOCA

Yield – 12 verrines

Fruit gelee
Passion fruit juice – 80 gms
Fresh orange juice, fresh – 80 gms
Caster sugar – 30 gms
Gelatin powder – 8 gms

Coconut tapioca
Tapioca pearls – 60 gms
Coconut milk, unsweetened – 180 gms
Caster sugar – 60 gms
Fleur de sel – a pinch

Chia seeds
Chia seeds – 25 gms
Hot water – 50 gms

Fruit curd
Passion fruit purée – 40 gms
Mango purée – 40 gms
Orange juice – 40 gms
Lemon juice – 10 gms
Caster sugar – 150 gms
Fleur de sel – a pinch
Egg yolks – 7
Unsalted butter – 450 gms
Gelatin powder – 4 gms

Fruit gelee: Soften gelatin in 40 gms cold water. Bring orange and passion fruit juice and sugar to a boil for 5 seconds, and remove the pan from the heat. Stir in the gelatin until it has dissolved. Portion the gelee into fleximolds using a funnel gun, filling the cavities up to the top and then refrigerate.

Coconut tapioca: Place the tapioca in a small pot and cover it with cold water. Bring the mixture to a boil and strain out the resulting liquid. Return the tapioca to the pot, cover with fresh cold water, and repeat the process about four times or until the tapioca is translucent. Rinse the tapioca in cold water to stop it being cooked further. Put the tapioca in a bowl with the coconut milk, sugar and salt. Mix until the sugar has dissolved. The tapioca must be made just before assembling the dessert to prevent it from clumping.

Chia seeds: Combine hot water and chia seeds in a small cup and let it sit for at least one hour uncovered at room temperature before using.

Fruit curd: Soften gelatin in 20 gms cold water. In a small saucepan, combine the mango and passion fruit purée and orange and lemon juice and bring to a boil. Meanwhile, place the sugar, salt, and egg yolks in a bowl and whisk. Pour the boiling passion fruit mix into the yolk mixture while whisking vigorously. Place on top of the bain-marie and stir occasionally until the curd thickens. Cook till it is 90°C, take the curd off the bain-marie and stir in the butter in small batches. Make sure it is all melted, and then stir in the gelatin till completely dissolved. Strain the curd through a fine-mesh sieve into a bowl and cover it with cling film. Let it cool to room temperature, stirring every five minutes.

Once the fruit curd is cool, pipe in to fill one-fourth of the glasses. Top with coconut tapioca, reaching almost to the top of the glass. Unmold the orange and passion fruit gelee and put on top along with the chia seeds.

Tapioca pearls are usually neutral in flavour plus gel easily, and are often used as a thickening agent in foods.

MATCHA & RASPBERRY ICE CREAM

Yield – 8/10 servings

Matcha ice cream
Milk – 565 gms
Cream, 35% – 175 gms
Matcha powder – 20 gms
Caster sugar – 120 gms
Milk powder – 55 gms
Atomized glucose – 55 gms
Ice cream stabilizer – 5 gms

Raspberry ice cream
Milk – 575 gms
Caster sugar – 175 gms
Ice cream stabilizer – 5 gms
Milk powder – 110 gms
Atomized glucose – 60 gms
Cream, 35% – 240 gms
Frozen raspberry puree – 350 gms

Topping
Raspberry flakes, freeze dried
Cherry flakes, freeze dried

Matcha ice cream: Mix stabilizer in 20 gms sugar and keep aside. Heat the milk, cream and Matcha powder to 40°C. Add remaining sugar, milk powder and glucose powder. Add stabilizer – sugar mix and cook to 85°C. Mix and cool to 4°C. Mature for at least 4 hours or preferably overnight in a covered container in the refrigerator. Use hand blender to mix then churn until the ice cream gets the desired consistency. Remove from the ice cream machine, and transfer to silicone molds and freeze.

Raspberry ice cream: Mix stabilizer with 20 gms sugar and keep aside. Heat milk, remaining sugar, milk powder, glucose powder and cream to 40°C. Add the stabilizer and sugar mix and cook to 85°C. Mix and cool to 4°C. Mature for at least 4 hours or preferably overnight in a covered container in the refrigerator. Add raspberry puree and use hand blender to mix and then churn in an ice cream machine till the ice cream gets the desired consistency. Transfer to silicone molds and freeze.

Sprinkle raspberry flakes on top of raspberry ice cream and cherry flakes over the Matcha ice cream.

SUMMER IN PARADISE

Yield – 8 servings

Cream cheese sorbet
Water – 150 gms
Caster sugar – 100 gms
Zest of ½ lemon, finely grated
Cream cheese – 250 gms
Sour cream – 120 gms
Plain yogurt – 120 gms

Yogurt cake
All-purpose flour – 350 gms
Baking powder – 1 tbsp
Fleur de sel – a pinch
Eggs – 3
Caster sugar – 300 gms
Vegetable oil – 90 gms
Greek yogurt – 175 gms
Vanilla extract – 1 tsp

Topping
Kiwi fruits
Mint sprigs
Pistachios, slivered
Lime fruit jelly

Cream cheese sorbet: Boil sugar and water, stir to dissolve the sugar. Remove from heat and add lemon zest. Cool in refrigerator. In a large mixing bowl, using a hand blender to combine the cream cheese, sour cream, and yogurt. Add the sugar syrup and blend well. Cover the bowl and refrigerate for at least four hours. Churn in an ice cream machine. Pour in any shaped silicone mold and freeze.

Yogurt cake: In a medium bowl, sift together the flour, baking powder and salt and whisk until mixed. Set aside. In a large bowl, whisk together the eggs, sugar, and oil until blended. Whisk in the yogurt and vanilla extract. Stir in the sifted flour mixture, one-third at a time, mixing just until combined. Scrape the batter into the greased 23 x 10 cm loaf pan and bake at 170°C in a preheated oven for about 40 to 50 minutes or until a skewer inserted into the centre of the cake comes out clean. Cool the cake in the pan while set on a wire rack for about 15 minutes. Unmold the cake onto the rack and cool completely.

Topping: Cut slices of cake, spread some lime fruit jelly and kiwi slices and top with sorbet. Sprinkle with pistachios and mint sprigs.

CHOCOLATE & RASPBERRY DIVINITY

Yield – 4 servings

Crumble
Szechuan pepper, finely ground – 8 gms
Caster sugar – 120 gms
All-purpose flour – 200 gms
Cocoa powder – 65 gms
Baking powder – 4 gms
Maldon sea salt – 2 gms
Unsalted butter – 190 gms

Chocolate cake
All-purpose flour – 90 gms
Brown sugar – 70 gms
Cocoa powder – 6 gms
Baking soda – 1.5 gms
Unsalted butter, melted – 50 gms
Cream, 35% – 50 gms
Milk – 50 gms
Golden syrup – 35 gms
Dark chocolate, 60-70%, melted – 50 gms

Pepper mousse
Milk – 105 gms
Szechuan pepper – 6 gms
Caster sugar – 65 gms
Egg yolks – 3
Milk chocolate – 215 gms
Dark chocolate, 60-70% – 110 gms
Raspberry puree – 45 gms
Cream, 35%, softly whipped – 215 gms

Raspberry sauce
Raspberry puree – 250 gms
Neutral gel – 50 gms

Raspberry sorbet
Water (A) – 445 gms
Caster sugar – 315 gms
Atomized glucose – 235 gms
Sorbet stabilizer – 5 gms
Raspberry puree – 1165 gms
Water (B) – 15 gms

Sesame tuiles
Icing sugar – 60 gms
Unsalted butter – 20 gms
Honey – 30 gms
Water – 15 ml
Fleur de sel – a pinch
Black sesame seeds – 80 gms
All-purpose flour – 20 gms

Crumble: Mix the flour, cocoa powder, pepper and baking powder in the bowl of a stand mixer and then add the rest of the ingredients and mix to make a crumble. Divide between silicone mats and bake at 165°C in a preheated oven for approximately 10-20 minutes.

Soft chocolate cake: Combine all the dry ingredients in a bowl and mix well. Combine butter, cream, milk and golden syrup in another bowl and whisk together until the golden syrup has dissolved. Pour the wet ingredients on to the dry ingredients and whisk briefly until it comes together to a batter. Add the chocolate and combine. Pour into greased 20 cm square pan and bake at 180°C in a preheated oven for 20-30 minutes. Cut into cubes.

Pepper mousse: Bring the milk to a boil. Add the pepper and a low to infuse for 20 minutes. Strain the milk. Put the milk, egg yolks and sugar in a pan and cook to 85°C, while whisking continuously. Pour over chocolate and mix. Add raspberry puree and emulsify with hand blender. Fold in the cream and pipe into silicone molds of your choice and freeze.

Raspberry sauce: Mix the ingredients and store in the refrigerator.

Raspberry sorbet: Mix half the sugar with stabiliser. Heat water (A) at 25°C, add rest of the sugar and glucose. At 45°C, add the stabiliser and sugar mix and cook to 85°C. Refrigerate and cool to 4°C. Add the puree and water (B) and mix with hand blender. Let it rest in refrigerator for at least four hours. Churn in ice cream machine and freeze in quenelle silicone molds.

Sesame tuiles: Place icing sugar, butter, honey, water and salt in a saucepan and bring to a boil for a minute over moderate heat while stirring. Remove pan from heat and stir in sesame seeds and flour until mixture is thoroughly combined. Cool to room temperature. Spread on a parchment lined baking tray. Bake tuiles at 180°C in a preheated oven, for 7-8 minutes. Cool and store in airtight container.

Remove the mousse from silicone mold and arrange crumble and sesame tuiles on top. Pipe raspberry sauce on top of the cake cubes and arrange on a platter. Serve with a quenelle of sorbet.

CHOCOLATE & RASPBERRY DIVINITY

FROZEN MOJITO

Yield – 4/6 servings

Sorbet
Caster sugar – 120 gms
Atomised glucose – 60 gms
Maltodextrin – 90 gms
Sorbet stabilizer – 4 gms
Purified water – 450 gms
Lime puree – 160 gms
Rum – 120 gms

Mint jelly
Water – 250 gms
Brown sugar – 30 gms
Mint leaves – 10 gms
Agar agar – 4 gms
Green colour
Gelatin – 2 gms

Topping
Mint sprigs
White rum

Sorbet: Mix the sugar, glucose, Maltodextrin and the stabilizer together. Heat the water to 65°C, add the dry ingredients and heat further to 85°C. Add the lime puree and the rum. Mature the mix for at least four hours in the refrigerator. Churn in the ice cream machine and freeze.

Mint jelly: Soften gelatin in 10 gms cold water and keep aside. Bring the water and sugar to the boil. Add fresh mint leaves and allow to soak for 10 minutes. Pass through a fine sieve and add the Agar agar. Bring the sieved fluid back to a boil. Add a little green colour and the gelatin. Mix and immediately pour the jelly into a shallow dish so that a 1 cm thick layer is formed. Allow to cool. Cut the mint jelly into cubes and keep in the freezer.

Half fill the glass dishes with sorbet and place in the freezer. Add a few cubes of mint jelly. Fill up the glass dishes to within 1 cm of the rim with another layer of sorbet and return to freezer.

Decorate each glass dish with some cubes of mint jelly, a sprig of fresh mint and a pipette filled with rum.

CHOCOLATE & AMARETTI PUDDING

Yield – 4/6 servings

Amaretti biscuits
Egg whites – 2
Caster sugar – 170 gms
Almond flour – 170 gms
Amaretto liquor – 15 ml

Pudding
Milk – 100 gms
Cream, 35% – 100 gms
Unsalted butter – 50 gms
Dark chocolate, 60-70% – 200 gms
Egg yolks – 2
Icing sugar – 100 gms
Amaretti biscuits – 150 gms (recipe on right)
Amaretto liqueur – 100 ml

Amaretti biscuits: Beat the egg whites until firm. Mix the sugar and the almond flour gently into it. Add the amaretto liquor and fold in gently until you have a smooth paste. Pipe small heaps of the mixture approximately 4 cm apart on a parchment lined and greased baking tray. Bake biscuits at 170°C in a preheated oven, for approximately 15 minutes, until golden brown. Leave to cool then store in an airtight container.

Pudding: In a medium saucepan, heat the milk, cream and butter until just before it boils. Take off the heat and stir in the chocolate until it has completely melted. Leave to cool for about 10 minutes. Once cooled, beat in the egg yolks and icing sugar.

Break up the Amaretti biscuits into your serving glasses and pour a trickle of Amaretto in each glass and then spoon in the pudding. Leave to set in the refrigerator overnight. Serve with Amaretti biscuits and a chilled glass of Amaretto.

SUMMER FIESTA

Yield – 10/12 servings

Lemon curd
Lemon juice – 90 ml
Eggs – 2
Egg yolks – 3
Caster sugar – 55 gms
Unsalted butter – 100 gms

Oat streusel
Rolled oats, crushed – 85 gms
All-purpose flour – 30 gms
Caster sugar – 15 gms
Salt – ¼ tsp
Baking soda – ⅛ tsp
Unsalted butter – 55 gms

Italian meringue
Caster sugar – 200 gms
Water – 80 ml
Liquid glucose – 20 gms
Egg whites – 3

Mango sorbet
Water (A) – 445 gms
Caster sugar – 315 gms
Atomised glucose – 235 gms
Sorbet stabiliser – 5 gms
Mango puree – 560 gms
Water (B) – 20 gms

Flavoured syrup
Sugar – 200 gms
Water – 500 ml
Vermouth – 100 ml
Verbena leaves – 5 gms

Melon with vacuum
Melon – 400 gms
Flavoured syrup
(recipe on next page)

Topping
Passion Fruit seeds
White chocolate decorations

Lemon curd: Mix eggs, egg yolks, sugar and lemon juice in a bowl. Whisk the egg mix over the bain-marie until thick and only then add the butter, whisking until incorporated. Store in an airtight container in the refrigerator until ready to use.

Oat streusel: Mix all the dry ingredients together in a mixing bowl. Melt the butter in a pan, then pour into the dry mixture and incorporate. Place mix in a shallow baking tray lined with parchment paper and bake at 160°C in a preheated oven for 10 minutes or until lightly golden.

Italian meringue: Boil the sugar, water and glucose to 120°C. Whisk the egg whites to soft peaks. Pour the hot sugar mixture in slowly and keep whisking until cool.

Mango sorbet: Mix half the sugar with stabiliser. Heat water (A) at 25°C, add rest of the sugar and glucose. At 45°C mix the stabilizer and sugar and cook to 85°C. Refrigerate and cool to 4°C. Add the puree and water (B) and mix with hand blender. Let it rest in refrigerator for at least 4 hours. Churn in ice cream machine and freeze in decorative silicone molds.

Flavoured syrup: Boil sugar, water and verbena leaves. Infuse for 15 minutes. Cool and add vermouth.

Melon with vacuum: Make juliennes of the melon. Mix with flavoured syrup and pack in a sous-vide bag. Vacuum seal the bag and cool in refrigerator for at least three hours. Strain the melon juliennes before using.

Assembly: Place a few teaspoons of Italian meringue on the back of a flat pan, then turn the pan with the meringue attached to it onto a serving plate. While holding the plate with one hand, press the pan down onto the plate and then lift up the pan in one quick stroke. Blow torch the meringue and on it arrange all the components and topping as desired.

Chocolate Epiphany

CHOCOLATES

SPICE TRUFFLES

Yield – 25 truffles

Cream, 35% – 150 gms
Invert sugar – 40 gms
Unsalted butter – 65 gms
Dark chocolate, 60-70%, chopped – 315 gms
Lemon juice – 20 gms
Ginger juice – 20 gms
Tempered dark chocolate, for covering
Cocoa powder, for rolling

These decadent truffles are the perfect after-dinner indulgence.

Bring the cream to a boil with the invert sugar. Cool to 85°C. Pour onto the chocolate and stir in the centre with a rubber spatula to create an elastic texture with a glossy appearance. Add the diced butter. Blend well to perfect the emulsion. Finish by adding the lemon juice and the fresh ginger juice and mix with hand blender. Cover with cling film and leave for about two hours at room temperature. Put mixture in piping bag and with a plain tip, pipe into rounds on parchment lined tray. Let these set at room temperature overnight.

Coat with tempered dark chocolate and put on a tray with cocoa powder. Roll the balls with a chocolate fork and leave to set. Be careful not to leave the mark of the fork. Use a sieve to remove excess cocoa powder.

CHOCOLATE HAZELNUT DELIGHTS

Yield – 25/30 delights

Hazelnut spread
Hazelnut praline – 60 gms
Hazelnut paste – 30 gms
Milk chocolate, melted – 35 gms
Milk powder – 7.5 gms
Unsalted butter – 5 gms
Grapeseed oil – 5 gms
Fleur de sel – a pinch

Chocolate hazelnut cups
Dark chocolate, 65-70%, melted – 100 gms
Hazelnut spread – 110 gms
Hazelnut powder – 25 gms
Paillete feuilletine – 1 tbsp
Hazelnuts, toasted – 50 gms
Chocolate bits – 1 tbsp
Cocoa nibs, roasted – 1 tbsp

Paillete feuilletine is crushed up pieces of crêpes dentelles, or lacey super-thin crêpes and can be bought or made at home.

Hazelnut spread: Mix praline and hazelnut paste. Add milk powder, butter, salt and melted chocolate. Mix and add the oil in the end.

Chocolate hazelnut cups: Using small, clean paintbrush, paint chocolate thickly inside 2.5 cm foil cases. Place cases on tray; refrigerate for about 5 minutes or until chocolate sets. Peel away the foil cases.

Combine spread and hazelnut powder in small bowl; spoon mixture into a piping bag fitted with 1.5 cm fluted tube and pipe on the chocolate cups. Divide feuilletine and hazelnuts among chocolate cups.

Sprinkle with chocolate bits, cocoa nibs and paillete feuilletine.

RASPBERRY PRALINES

Yield – 50 pralines

Ganache
Cream, 35% – 125 gms
Raspberry puree – 150 gms
Dark chocolate, 60-70%, chopped – 335 gms
Invert sugar – 65 gms
Unsalted butter, diced – 70 gms
Orange blossom water – 15 gms

Molding
Dark chocolate, 60-70%, tempered

Decoration
Pink sugar or glitter

Ganache: Bring the cream to a boil with the invert sugar, cool to 85°C and gradually pour onto the chocolate. Stir in the centre with a rubber spatula to create a smooth emulsion. Add in the warm raspberry pulp. Add butter, then the orange blossom water. Mix with a hand blender. Cool to 28/29°C and keep ready to pour in a piping bag to fill the molds.

Molding: Clean the mold with a cotton bud dipped in vodka. Pour the tempered chocolate in the mold, give a few taps on the mold to get rid of air bubbles, then scrape the top of the mold to remove extra chocolate. Turn the mold upside down to remove the excess chocolate leaving a thin shell in the mold. Scrape again to clean the top of the mold.

Pipe the molded bonbons with the ganache. Make sure that no ganache comes on the side of the molded chocolate. Once the molds are filled, give a little bit of a tap, to make the ganache relax and allow it to become flat. Allow the ganache to crystallize for a minimum of 24 hours before sealing the shells.

De-crystallize the shells very slightly using a blowtorch. Pour a another coat of tempered chocolate to cover ganache. Scrape the top of the mold again. Give the mold a little bit of a tap, just to make sure that no air bubbles. Allow the chocolate to crystallize for a few minutes in the refrigerator. Turn the mold upside down to take the bonbons out; give a little tap if necessary.

Decorate with pink glitter or pink sugar.

COFFEE & COOKIE CHOCOLATES

Yield – 25/30 chocolates

Crispy cookies
All-purpose flour – 350 gms
Caster sugar – 200 gms
Fine semolina – 175 gms
Dark chocolate, 60-70% – 250 gms
Egg – 1
Unsalted butter, soft – 375 gms
Hazelnut crocant – 250 gms
Baking powder – ¼ tsp
Fleur de sel – a pinch
Seeds of 1 Vanilla bean

Coffee mousse
Unsalted butter – 250 gms
Fondant – 200 gms
Dark chocolate, 60-70% – 400 gms
Instant coffee – 3 gms

Enrobing
Dark chocolate, 60-70%, tempered

Crispy cookies: Sift flour and baking powder in the bowl of a stand mixer. Add the other ingredients and knead with a dough hook. Leave to rest overnight in the refrigerator. Roll to 4 mm thickness and cut into 3 cm rounds. Put on a parchment lined tray and bake at 150°C in a preheated oven for 10 minutes. Let it cool before use.

Coffee mousse: Stir in the butter with the fondant until fluffy. Fold in the tempered chocolate. Add coffee and mix carefully. Pipe on top of crispy cookie. Leave overnight in a cool place.

Enrobe with tempered dark chocolate.

INTENSE HOT CHOCOLATE

Yield – 4 servings

Dark chocolate, 60-70% – 120 gms
Milk – 500 ml
Cocoa powder – 25 gms
Caster sugar – 30 gms
Cocoa powder, for sprinkling

Using a single origin dark chocolate could add an extra kick to the drink.

Grate the chocolate and set aside. Heat the milk, cocoa, and sugar in a pan. Remove from heat, add chocolate and whisk the mixture at high speed for at least 2 minutes.

When the hot chocolate is very frothy, serve immediately in four large cups. Sprinkle cocoa powder on top.

FRUIT & CHOCOLATE BARS

Yield – 10 bars

White chocolate – 250 gms
Dark chocolate, 60-70% – 125 gms
Cranberries and cherries, dried
Pistachios, shelled, coarsely chopped
Pink peppercorns

Temper white and dark chocolate separately. Chop one of the chocolates and melt it slowly over a bain-marie. When the temperature of the chocolate reaches 55°C – 58°C for dark / 45°C – 50°C for white, pour two-thirds of each onto a marble slab. Keep the remaining third warm, either over the bain-marie or in a warm place, but not over direct heat

Using a flexible spatula and a metal spatula, keep spreading and turning the chocolate until the recommended temperatures are reached. Dark chocolate must reach 28°C – 29°C and white chocolate should reach 26°C – 27°C.

Return the melted, stirred chocolate to a separate mixing bowl and gradually pour in the warm chocolate that was set aside until it reaches a temperature of 31°C – 32 °C for dark, and 28°C – 29°C for white chocolate. Pour the dark and white chocolate alternatively in any shaped mold of choice.

Shake gently to level, then quickly dot with dried cranberries, cherries, pistachios and pink peppercorns. Allow to set.

MOCCABEAN BONBONS

Yield – 25/30 bonbons

Filling
Caster sugar – 500 gms
Water – 175 gms
Liquid glucose – 15 gms
Instant coffee – 15 gms
Dark rum – 50 ml
Alcohol 98% – 50 ml
Cinnamon stick – 1
Green cardamom – 10

Molding
Dark chocolate, 60-70%, tempered

Sealing the bonbons is key to preserving the alcohol and flavour.

Filling: Boil sugar, water, cinnamon stick and cardamom. Cover and let it infuse for approximately 10 minutes. Take the spices out and add instant coffee. Add glucose and heat it up to 106°C. Cool the syrup to 50°C and add alcohol. Repour from one container to another a few times. Do not stir with a spoon.

Molding: Fill the mold with tempered chocolate. Use the scraper to tap the sides of the molds to remove any air bubbles. Turn the mold upside down and tap with a scraper again. Turn the mold right way up and scrape off the excess chocolate with the scraper. Place the mold upside down on a parchment-lined tray. Leave it to set for about 10-15 minutes in a cool, dry place.

Fill in the liquor solution into the chocolate lined cavities and leave it overnight. First spray with tempered chocolate on top of the liquor solution and then seal with tempered chocolate. Allow the chocolate to crystallize for a few minutes in the refrigerator. Turn the mold over to take the bonbons out; give a little tap to the mold if necessary.

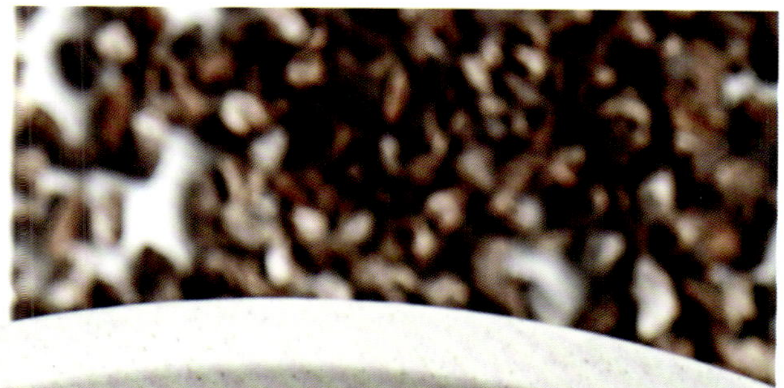

TELLICHERRY PRALINES

Yield – 25/30 pralines

Fruit jelly
Red pepper puree – 100 gms
Raspberry puree – 40 gms
Water – 65 gms
Pectin NH – 6 gms
Caster sugar (A) – 20 gms
Caster sugar (B) – 225 gms
Citric acid – 2 gms
Liquid Glucose – 65 gms

Tellicherry pepper ganache
Cream, 35% – 85 gms
Invert sugar – 35 gms
Sorbitol – 40 gms
Unsalted butter, soft – 50 gms
Cocoa butter – 5 gms
Dark chocolate, 60-70% – 250 gms
Tellicherry pepper – 4 gms

Enrobing
Dark chocolate, 60-70%, tempered

Fruit jelly: Warm up the red pepper and raspberry puree with water upto 50°C. Mix pectin with sugar (A) and add to puree mix. Give a boil and add sugar (B) and glucose gradually and heat it to 107°C. Add the citric acid dissolved in 2 gms water, mix and immediately pour into the ganache frame.

Tellicherry pepper ganache: Heat up the cream, invert sugar, sorbitol and pepper to just before boiling point. Remove from heat, cover with cling film and leave to infuse for 10 minutes. Strain onto chocolate and cocoa butter. Let it sit undisturbed for 2 minutes. Now mix with a spatula. Add butter and make an emulsion with a hand blender.

Pour over the fruit jelly into the ganache frame. Leave to set overnight. Pour a thin layer of tempered chocolate on the upper side. Turn it over and cut into square of 2.5 cm x 2.5 cm. Enrobe with tempered dark chocolate and decorate as desired.

COFFEE PRALINES

Yield – 25 pralines

Cream, 35% – 85 gms
Liquid glucose – 10 gms
Instant coffee powder – 8 gms
Fleur de sel – a pinch
Honey – 15 gms
Milk chocolate – 240 gms
Unsalted butter, soft – 40 gms

Enrobing
Milk chocolate, tempered
Chocolate coffee beans

Bring the cream, glucose, coffee, salt and honey to the boil. Cool to 80°C. Pour over milk chocolate. Do not stir for 5 minutes. Emulsify with a spatula stirring from the centre. To get a smooth, shiny ganache, its better to use hand blender. Fold in the butter and blend again. Immediately spread the ganache evenly in a frame. Leave to crystallize in the refrigerator for approximately one hour. Using a guitar cutter or a sharp knife, cut to the desired size.

Allow to return to room temperature before enrobing with tempered milk chocolate. Garnish immediately with a chocolate coffee bean.

CORIANDER PRALINES

Yield – 25/30 pralines

Filling
Caster sugar – 200 gms
Sorbitol powder – 15 gms
Water – 75 gms
Hazelnuts, roasted – 350 gms
Coriander seeds, roasted – 10 gms
Milk powder – 15 gms
Milk chocolate, melted – 120 gms
Cocoa butter, melted – 60 gms

Molding
Dark chocolate, 60-70 %, tempered

Filling: Heat sugar, sorbitol and water to 185°C. Remove from heat and add the hazelnuts and coriander seeds. Spread on silicone mat and cool. Make a fine paste in a heavy duty mixer. Stir in milk chocolate, cocoa butter, and milk powder and mix well again. Pour in a bowl and stir continuously or temper on a granite slab to 26°C.

Molding: Fill the mold with tempered chocolate. Use the scraper to tap the sides of the mold to remove any air bubbles. Turn the mold upside down and tap with a scraper again. Turn mold back the right way up and scrape off the excess chocolate with the scraper. Now place the mold upside down on a parchment-lined tray. Leave it to set for about 10-15 minutes in a cool, dry place.

Pipe the filling into each cavity, leaving a small gap for the capping. Leave it overnight in a cool place. To cap, pour more tempered dark chocolate over the top of the mold. Level of with a scraper. Leave the mold to fully set for at least 2-3 hours in a cool, dry place. Once set, twist the mold to loosen the chocolates. Turn it upside down and tap gently so that the chocolates drop out of the mold.

HELPFUL NOTES

Tempering Chocolate

Tempering chocolate is an essential step for making smooth, glossy, evenly colored coating for your dipped chocolates. Tempering prevents the dull greyish color and waxy texture that happens when the cocoa fat separates out.

"Tempering by Seeding" is the easiest and quickest way to temper chocolate. Chop the chocolate into small pieces. Set aside about 25 to 30 per cent of the chocolate. Place the remaining 70 to 75 per cent of chopped chocolate in a microwave-safe bowl and microwave on half-power, being very careful to stir the mixture every minute until it is almost completely melted, which should take about four to five minutes.

Remove the bowl of chocolate from the microwave and check the temperature of the melted chocolate – it should be between:

· Dark Chocolate: 46–48°C
· Milk Chocolate: 40–45°C
· White Chocolate: 37–40°C

Start adding chopped chocolate you set aside, to the melted chocolate. Stir in the chocolate bits continuously until the desired temperature (see below) is reached and the bits have dissolved completely.. Your chocolate should now be tempered.

· Dark chocolate should be between 31°C–32°C

Milk and white chocolates should be between 29–30°C

Make sure to stir the tempered chocolate and check the temperature during the time you are using it for dipping or molding. You can put the tempered chocolate mass in the microwave for 10–15 seconds at half-power if the temperature starts to drop. Just make sure that you don't raise the temperature above 32°C or you will lose your temper and have to start over again.

Baking "Blind"

This is about partially, or sometimes completely, baking the tart crust before you add the filling. As the crust bakes, pockets of steam cause the layers of pastry to puff up – not useful when one's goal is to fill the pie with something else. The solution is to line the unbaked tart crust with parchment or aluminum foil and weight it down with something so that the bottom doesn't puff and the sides don't slouch. You can find special pie weights for this job, but you can also just use dry beans.

Once the crust is cooked and the edges turn golden, remove the weights and let the crust cook a little longer on its own. For a partially baked crust, you want the bottom to look dry and flaky, but still pale. For a fully baked crust, the bottom should turn light golden.

Preheating the Oven

For any kind of baking, the oven must be preheated to the proper temperature. Since this can take a while, it is best to start the preheating about 10 minutes before baking.

MODERNIST INGREDIENTS

Agar Agar
A clear, tasteless gelling and thickening agent. Derived from seaweed, it has been used in Asia for centuries. Agar agar has recently attracted avant garde chefs due to its flexibility with heat. Will form gels at 31°C and does not melt below 58°C.

Carrageenan
It comes in three different varieties: iota, kappa, and lambda. Iota carageenan makes soft, elastic gels. Kappa carrageenan makes firm, brittle gels. Lambda carrageenan thickens liquids but does not cause them to gel. All three kinds are derived from seaweed; carrageenan takes its name from a fishing village in Ireland, where the seaweed has traditionally been used to make pudding.

Isomalt
This a sugar substitute, a type of sugar alcohol used primarily as a sweetener, bulking, anti-caking and glazing agent in low-calorie sweets, desserts, cakes chocolates, ice creams and baked goods. It has little to no impact on blood sugar levels, and does not stimulate the release of insulin.

Locust Bean Gum
Also called carob bean gum, is extracted from the outer coating of the carob seed. It is a hydrocolloid thickener and gelling agent. It forms a food reserve for the seeds and helps to retain water under arid conditions.

Low Acyl Gellan
This gelling agent can be used alone or in a combination to produce a variety of interesting textures. It quickly sets when under its gelling temperature. It provides remarkable stability, high gel strength, heat stable, sparkling clarity and excellent flavour release.

Maltodextrin
It is derived from tapioca starch using natural enzymatic process, and is used as a thickener, bulking agent and adsorbent. It's low density and large surface area make it good for making dry powders and pastes from oils and other liquids (such as alcohol).

Soy Lecithin
A natural phospholipid from soybean, it is partially water-soluble, an emulsifying agent that helps fat and water stay together. Therefore, it is often added to foods, such as chocolate, cheese and dressing. It has health benefits such as reducing cholesterol level.

Versawhip
A modified soy protein, it exhibits exceptionally consistent whipping performance and is widely used in sugar confectionery products. Used to replace egg albumin or gelatin with the advantage of having no egg flavor at all and producing more stable foams. It can be used for hot or cold foams.

Xantana
A long chain polysacharide composed of the sugars glucose, mannose, and glucuronic acid. It is used as a thickener in sauces, as an agent in ice cream that prevents ice crystals from forming, and as a fat substitute that adds the "mouth feel" of fat without the calories.

INDEX

NOTES